IKTOMI AND THE DUCKS
and Other Sioux Stories

RETOLD BY
ZITKALA-ŠA

FOREWORD BY
AGNES M. PICOTTE

Introduction by P. Jane Hafen

University of Nebraska Press
Lincoln and London

CONTENTS

v

P. JANE HAFEN

Introduction

In 1901, twenty-five-year-old Zitkala-Ša, also called Gertrude Simmons (1876–1938, Yankton Sioux), was at a crest of public exposure. She had won an award for her speaking abilities and had taught at Carlisle Indian School in Pennsylvania. She had proved herself an accomplished musician and had performed for the president of the United States. She was the author of memoirs and short stories in popular American periodicals and had a commission to write a book of Indian legends. She was poised to begin studying with a prestigious violinist in Boston, and she was engaged to marry Dr. Carlos Montezuma (1866–1923), the noted Apache political activist.

The book, *Iktomi and the Ducks and Other Sioux Stories*, (originally published as *Old Indian Legends* by McGinn and Company), appeared as scheduled, but nearly everything else in Zitkala-Ša's life took a different direction. She did not pursue a musical career, she did not marry Montezuma (she later married fellow Yankton Sioux Raymond T. Bonnin instead), and she appeared to lose interest in her literary career. She disappeared from the public eye for fifteen years, emerging in 1916 as a political activist in her own right when elected secretary of the Society of American Indians. Zitkala-Ša's attention turned from storytelling to expository writing and political activism, to speech-giving and congressional testifying. She lived an active life in Washington DC, working directly on behalf of Indian peoples until her death in 1938.

Agnes M. Picotte's foreword to the 1985 University of Nebraska edition of this book is thorough in its early biographical sketch of Zitkala-Ša and in its discussion of the role of *ohunkankans* (stories) and the Iktomi trickster in Sioux society. Picotte also places the volume in the context of the writings of Zitkala-Ša's Sioux contemporaries: Charles Eastman (1858–1939), Luther Standing Bear (1868-1939), and Ella Deloria (1888–1971). The rhetorical positioning of *Iktomi and the Ducks and Other Sioux Stories* and some of the critical responses to the writings of Zitkala-Ša still deserve assessment.

Zitkala-Ša leaves Boston early in 1901. She goes home "to divide [her] time between teaching and getting story material" (Zitkala-Ša 1901). Her methodology for gathering material is not documented. However, if she followed the pattern she used for "The Witch Woman" and "Squirrel Man and His Double," she first collected and wrote the story in the Dakota language (Hafen 2001, 71–85). Then she translated and shaped the story for her audience, presumably non-Indians. According to Jeanne Smith, Zitkala-Ša transformed several of the stories for publication in *Iktomi and the Ducks*, most notably "Dance in a Buffalo Skull," where she "represents this tale about the threat of devouring colonialism as a ghost story, charging the inherited narrative with more serious political implications" (Smith 1994, 50). Smith makes additional comparisons between Ella Deloria's "scientific" versions of several stories and Zitkala-Ša's literary presentations and suggests that those presentations have a distinct purpose. The heroic acts of Blood Clot Boy and the stories themselves are enhanced to "resona[te] in the context of the 1901 publication, when the allotment act and the mission boarding schools were gigantically, indifferently swallowing up Lakota [*sic*] lands and culture" (Smith 1994, 50).

The political implications of the stories are apparent in Zitkala-Ša's simple rhetorical style. She assumes, without apology, that the reader will enter into the nonce world she asserts. She adds details to give tribal context to the stories' characters, such as Iktomi the trickster, but does not allow for a reader's disbelief. The first story, "Iktomi and the Ducks," begins: "Iktomi is a spider fairy. He wears brown deerskin leggins with long soft fringes on either side, and tiny beaded moccasins on his feet. His long black hair is parted in the middle and wrapped with red, red bands" (p. 3). The traditional trickster is a humanized representation of the spider. There are no qualifiers in the description—he is not *like* a fairy or a spider; he *is* a spider fairy. His traditional dress and human appearance—"Iktomi dresses like a real Dakota brave"—enable him to interact with the other players in the story. Zitkala-Ša describes the trickster's character as "wily," "in mischief," and "naughty" (p. 4). Her Indian audience would already know Iktomi's persona, but she must explain him to her non-Indian readers (Lisa 1996, 61). Additionally, trickster stories have moral dimensions and are used to socialize proper behavior; since children are often the audience, the moral values being conveyed are pedagogically reinforced by both the tellers and the listeners.

In the case of "Iktomi and the Ducks," Iktomi's judgment is marred by his insatiable appetites. He wants to get his food by trickery rather than through "honest hunting" (p. 4). As with her other writings, Zitkala-Ša is acutely conscious of place. She makes clear that the story's setting is on the plains with tall grasses and marshy river bottoms. True to his nature, Iktomi tricks the ducks so he can satisfy his gluttony, but he then becomes impatient with the squeaking of a tree. His foot gets caught, and he is stuck in the tree as he watches a pack of wolves devour his catch, even the baking ducks hidden in the ashes. The wolves eat what Iktomi had selfishly kept for himself. Trickery and gluttony are punished as Iktomi remains stuck in the tree while his meal disappears.

Although Zitkala-Ša shapes the story for her audience, she also assumes the reader will accept the values portrayed by the story's characters. The conflict is not between Iktomi and the ducks but between Iktomi's desires and the larger corpus of moral values. Those moral values—condemnation of trickery and gluttony—might be seen as universal characteristics, yet Zitkala-Ša sets them within a specific tribal context. The lighthearted tone of the story combined with her prefatory remarks suggest that the story is directed toward children. The significance is not diminished just because the moral values are told within the framework of silly and exaggerated behaviors. The story entertains without didacticism.

Old Indian Legends remained in print until 1950. It has not received much critical attention despite the 1985 Bison Books reprint edition from the University of Nebraska Press (supported by the Dakota Indian Foundation and the Ella C. Deloria Project at the University of South Dakota, Vermillion). Nearly all literary and historical criticisms of Zitkala-Ša's work have focused on *American Indian Stories*, a 1921 compilation of magazine pieces published concurrently with *Old Indian Legends*. Although a number of critics mention *Old Indian Legends*, only Jeanne Smith examines these stories in her discussion of trickster discourse, and her essay soon switches to an assessment of *American Indian Stories* as well. *American Indian Stories*, particularly the autobiographical essays that have been widely anthologized, demonstrate Zitkala-Ša's conflicts with colonial powers. Her commentary on social justice walks a

fine line between sentimental engagement and outrage.
By railing against the imposing powers that deprive her of
her language, home, family, and traditions, she constructs
a modernist oppositional framework of binaries that se-
duces many critics. Diametrically opposed poles of tradition and modernity, of "pagan" beliefs and Christianity, and
of orality and literacy belie Zitkala-Ša's larger rhetorical
position. Such oppositions can end only in the tragedy of
the Vanishing American. Through the act of telling the
story itself, Zitkala-Ša reveals that she has transcended
those oppositions. She translated Dakota oral stories into
literary representations; she asserted traditional beliefs
while practicing a modern religion; she lived in a modern
world while celebrating traditional values. Rather than
being torn between two worlds, Zitkala-Ša relished and
thrived in both. Perhaps a more challenging critical position would examine how she maintained balance with an
assertion of survival. Perhaps that is also the challenge of
Iktomi and the Ducks. Because these traditional stories do
not assume a position of being defeated and colonized, the
obvious conflict is absent. Zitkala-Ša tells these stories with
a nod to her audience but disregards the imposition of ex-
ternal values. Rather than resistance through self-articu-
lation and social criticism, as found in "Impression of an
Indian Childhood," "The School Days of an Indian Girl,"
and "An Indian Teacher among Indians," Zitkala-Ša resists
by indigenizing and giving value to her tribal stories that
exist in their own cultural universe. Such a position is also
evident in many of the stories in *Dreams and Thunder*.

While the stories seem mostly encapsulated, the pref-
ace to *Old Indian Legends* is provocative. Zitkala-Ša begins: "These legends are relics of our country's once virgin
soil" (p. xv). With this verbal assault against colonial powers she sets a tone that throughout her life is consistently
found in her writings. She asserts that Indian stories have

inherent worth that should be recognized; no hierarchical or civilizing ladder divides the peoples. As she says, "The old legends of America belong quite as much to the blue-eyed little patriot as to the black-haired aborigine" (p. xvi). By demarcating physical characteristics she unmasks blatant racism. These stories are only eleven years removed from the Wounded Knee Massacre and, despite the official "closing of the frontier," many mainstream Americans still feared Indians and saw them as savages. She is righteously "demand[ing] a little respect. After all [the American aborigine] seems at heart much like other peoples" (p. xvi).

The power of language is self-reflective, as seen in her statement, "And now I have tried to transplant the native spirit of these tales—root and all—into the English language, since America in the last few centuries has acquired a second tongue" (p. xvi). She acknowledges the many layers of transformation—from orality to literacy, from Dakota to English—but in stating such she also "reminds the reader of the primacy of Native American[s] on American soil and reaffirms the validity of Native American culture, thereby redefining its relationship to the dominant culture" (Smith 1994, 47).

Zitkala-Ša continued to tell her stories. She wrote fourteen stories that remained unpublished until 2001 when they appeared in *Dreams and Thunder*. She continued to assert the value of Sioux culture in *The Sun Dance Opera* by expressing Sioux tradition in the highest art form of Western civilization. As she became involved in the real world politics of pan-Indianism and the workings of the federal government she reclaimed her given name, Gertrude Simmons Bonnin. Her writings, mostly speeches and editorials, returned to more obvious demands for justice for American Indians. Yet she remained influenced by the values in the stories she learned as a young woman. *Iktomi and the Ducks and Other Sioux Stories* remains timeless.

Introduction

WORKS CITED

Hafen, P. Jane, ed. 2001. *Dreams and Thunder: Stories, Poems, and the Sun Dance Opera by Zitkala-Ša*. Lincoln: University of Nebraska Press.

Lisa, Laurie. 1996. *The Life Story of Zitkala-Ša / Gertrude Simmons Bonnin: Writing and Creating a Public Image*. Ph.D. diss., Arizona State University.

Spack, Ruth. 2001. "Dis/engagement: Zitkala-Ša's Letters to Carlos Montezuma, 1901–1902." *MELUS* 26.1 (Spring): 172–204.

Smith, Jeanne. 1994. "'A Second Tongue': The Trickster's Voice in the Works of Zitkala-Ša." In *Tricksterism in Turn-of-the Century-American Literature: A Multicultural Perspective*, ed. Elizabeth Ammons and Annette White-Parks. 46–60. Hanover NH: University Press of New England.

Zitkala-Ša to Carlos Montezuma, February 20, 1901. The Papers of Carlos Montezuma M.D. 1983. [microfilm], Scholarly Resources, Wilmington DE.

PREFACE

THESE legends are relics of our country's once virgin soil. These and many others are the tales the little black-haired aborigine loved so much to hear beside the night fire.

For him the personified elements and other spirits played in a vast world right around the center fire of the wigwam.

Iktomi, the snare weaver, Iya, the Eater, and Old Double-Face are not wholly fanciful creatures.

There were other worlds of legendary folk for the young aborigine, such as " The Star-Men of the Sky," " The Thunder Birds Blinking Zigzag Lightning," and " The Mysterious Spirits of Trees and Flowers."

Under an open sky, nestling close to the earth, the old Dakota story-tellers have told me these legends. In both Dakotas, North and South, I have often listened to the same story told over again by a new story-teller.

While I recognized such a legend without the least difficulty, I found the renderings varying much in little incidents. Generally one helped the other in restoring some lost link in the original character of the tale. And now I have tried to transplant the native spirit of these tales — root and all — into the English language, since America in the last few centuries has acquired a second tongue.

The old legends of America belong quite as much to the blue-eyed little patriot as to the black-haired aborigine. And when they are grown tall like the wise grown-ups may they not lack interest in a further study of Indian folklore, a study which so strongly suggests our near kinship with the rest of humanity and points a steady finger toward the great brotherhood of mankind, and by which one is so forcibly impressed with the possible earnestness of life as seen through the teepee door! If it be true that much lies "in the eye of the beholder," then in the American aborigine as in any other race, sincerity of belief, though it were based upon mere optical illusion, demands a little respect.

After all he seems at heart much like other peoples.

ZITKALA-ŠA.

FOREWORD
By Agnes M. Picotte

In the early 1970s, I found a small book in the library of the University of Oregon, Eugene. It was by Zitkala-Ša. I recognized the name as Red Bird, since I am Lakota and my primary language is Lakota. I was truly delighted and surprised that Zitkala-Ša was able to write down the familiar legends in English.

That was my first introduction to Zitkala-Ša, whose American name was Gertrude Simmons Bonnin. I read her *Old Indian Legends* with much delight and was extremely proud that they were in print. Although she wrote these legends in 1902, they were as fresh as if they had just been written down. It was a great personal experience because I remember these legends or *ohunk-akan* (tales regarded as having some fictional elements) as told in my own primary language, Lakota, when only Lakota was spoken in my home.

I searched, to no avail, for her other book, *American Indian Stories,* printed in 1921. I did find, however, many of the stories and articles in magazines such as the *Atlantic Monthly, Harper's,* and *Everybody's Magazine.* Reading these, I began to know and appreciate the Yankton Sioux woman who spoke the Nakota dialect but had a Lakota name.

Zitkala-Ša impressed me as a great role model for American Indians interested in music, oratory, and writing. A master of language, she also became a violinist of some note, played other instruments, and sang solo and in

Foreword

choral groups. Her many talents, which she developed well, gave her prominence in the world about her. Her attachment to her roots in the primary Nakota culture gave her strength and endurance. She impressed me as a social reformer with a voice representing American Indian concerns and welfare.

A short biographical sketch of Zitkala-Ša from her birth, February 22, 1876, to the date of the publication of her book, *Old Indian Legends,* in 1902 will help us gain a better understanding of the significance of her contribution. A consideration of the conditions of the tribal society and the milieu from which she emerged will show how her book of legends fits into the body of Sioux oral tradition. A brief discussion of other Siouan authors of legends, myths, and animal stories will reveal a common purpose in publishing these works.

Born of a white father and a Yankton-Nakota mother called Tate I Yohin Win (Reaches for the Wind), whose American name was Ellen Simmons, Zitkala-Ša arrived in the same year as the Battle of the Little Big Horn. She spent her first eight years on the reservation before going away to a Quaker missionary school for Indians, the White's Manual Labor Institute in Wabash, Indiana. Zitkala-Ša returned to the reservation three years later and in the school year of 1888–89 enrolled in the Santee Normal Training School, which had been established at the Santee Agency in Nebraska almost a decade earlier.

During this time, the government was anxious to save the Indians through Christianity and civilization. Education was seen as the main tool for change, and children were the most logical subjects. Thus Zitkala-Ša was caught up in the dominant trend toward assimilation into the white society. Whether she knew it or not, she was being formed into a cultured, Christian lady, while being led to forget the old pagan ways.

Foreword

In 1891, Zitkala-Ša returned to White's Institute to complete her studies there. Available records on Zitkala-Ša show that in 1895 she was enrolled in another Quaker institution, Earlham College, in Richmond, Indiana. During her two years at Earlham, she led a very active extracurricular life, participating in musical programs. In these years, she also attended the Boston Conservatory School of Music. More importantly, she competed during this period in various oratorical contests, winning the second highest award in a statewide contest in 1896. In March of that year, her old school paper at the Santee Agency, *The Word Carrier,* printed her oratorical piece, "Side by Side," with much pride. (Later, in its February-March 1901 edition, the paper would denounce her article, "The Soft-Hearted Sioux," as morally bad.)

Illness caused her to leave her studies, but soon, in 1898, she was teaching at the Carlisle Indian School in Carlisle, Pennsylvania, which had been established in 1879 by Captain Richard Henry Pratt. Here, Zitkala-Ša, or Gertrude Simmons, spent several years teaching and performing with the orchestra.

At the turn of the century, Zitkala-Ša began writing and publishing her stories. In her twenties, she was increasingly aware of herself and her identity in the white world. She was an orator, musician, teacher, and now a writer. She was desirous of preserving and sharing what she had of her Nakota culture, and reinforced by her association with the Indian students at Carlisle, many of whom were Siouan, she undertook the writing of legends, many of which she learned in the Nakota dialect during her childhood.

The legends are told in an easy, engaging style with a certain dramatic power. Zitkala-Ša heard them as a child, and she carefully selected each story to appeal to her audiences of all ages, who were the children of the world.

Foreword

She was a most imaginative author, deeply concerned with beauty. She felt keenly throughout her formal education that she represented her race in everything she wrote. The 165 pages of *Old Indian Legends* contain fourteen stories filled with figures like Iktomi or Unktomi, the snare weaver, the cunning trickster whose tricks sometimes backfired. Iktomi-spider is an unconventional character who breaks all the rules of conduct and tradition. Many times he is purely foolish.

Eya also enters into the stories. He is the eater, the glutton who has magical powers. Able to deceive people in order to devour them, he is portrayed as a giant with a huge stomach and spindly legs. However, he is stupid and easily fooled. Another figure, Anuk-ite, or Old Double Face, is a giant with large, funnel-like ears. He is a cruel and evil person who delights in making children suffer. Lingering on the outskirts of camps waiting to snatch children away who might be out for any reason, he throws these children in his ears and takes them away to some secluded place to torture them. The Blood Clot boy is also a magical figure. He is a hero in the time of great need. The animal stories personify certain animals that are evil and others that are good.

Old Indian Legends draws on the oral tradition of storytelling in the Sioux Nation. Each narrator used his or her own style and personality to embellish each story according to his or her talents. The *ohunkankans* were told in the evening as everyone in the family went to bed, during the time between lying down and sleep. Any person in the family could be the storyteller, but mostly it was a grandparent or some other experienced person. Many times one distinguished for good *ohunkankans* was sought after, made a relative if not already one, and invited to be a guest for a month or any length of time so that he or she could tell *ohunkankans* to that particular family. Often a story could be continued for a few evenings or weeks on end. Thus the stories, customs, and legends were kept alive. Zitkala-Ša would help keep them alive by recording them.

The year after the publication of *Old Indian Legends,* in 1902, Zitkala-Ša married another Yankton-Nakota, Captain Raymond Bonnin, whom she had met on the reservation. To this union was born, in 1903, a boy, "Ohiya," meaning the "Winner," whose American name was also Raymond. The couple worked on various Indian reservations and finally ended up in Washington, D.C., helping American Indian people adjust to the white culture in whatever way they could.

In 1921, Zitkala-Ša published the second volume on which her literary reputation rests. The *American Indian Stories* are not entirely autobiographical. Many of them were told to her by people who had actually experienced the situations and circumstances they described. All of the stories were meant to inform white people about the American Indians and their unique condition, and a few reveal the turmoil, hurt, anger, and frustration felt by a sensitive, talented American Indian woman.

Gertie, as she was affectionately known, experienced conflicting emotions, and images of herself, her own Indian people, and also of the white people in her surroundings. Her intelligence, talents, and uniqueness earned for her a place in the limelight. Her accomplishments are impressive. Even so, Gertrude Bonnin felt so alone and so different at times that she felt compelled to go home to be with her mother on the Yankton Sioux Reservation. She needed to rest, renew her spirit, and to revitalize her true Nakota identity. Although she identified strongly with her Indian roots, Zitkala-Ša could

Foreword

never return to a grassroots Nakota stage again. She used
her knowledge of both the Indian and the white culture
mainly to help other American Indian people. Sadly, her
motives were distrusted many times by both sides due to
her tenuous bicultural condition.

It is my dream that every American Indian will have
the opportunity to read her books. For that matter, they
can be of value to all people as well.

Some of the same influences that drove Zitkala-Ša to
record Sioux legends, myths, and stories were at work in
contemporary and later Indian authors, and her position
as a pioneer who published early becomes clear in a
discussion of them. Probably the best known is Charles
Alexander Eastman (1858–1939), and others are Marie
McLaughlin (1842–?), Ella C. Deloria (1889–1971), and
Luther Standing Bear (1868–?).

Charles Eastman, a Santee Sioux, is the author of such
books of legends and stories as *Red Hunters and the
Animal People* (1904), *Old Indian Days* (1906), and *Wigwam Evenings—Sioux Tales Retold* (1909). His other
works are autobiographical. Like Zitkala-Ša, Eastman
was a product of the Santee Normal Training School and
had similar college experiences. Although he studied to be
a medical doctor, he, like Zitkala-Ša, felt the need to tell
his life story and to inform the white society about his
heritage. At the time he wrote the three books, he was
married, had a family, and was well into his forties. His
wife, Elaine Goodale Eastman, collaborated with him and
was of great assistance in editing the manuscripts. His
stories include the familiar Unktomi (in the Santee
dialect) and Iktomi (in the Teton dialect). The animal
stories concluded with a moral to be remembered; other
stories were about customs and traditions. He also wrote
for children.

Foreword

The Myths of the Sioux was published in 1916 by Marie McLaughlin. She was born in 1842 of a white father and a half-Indian mother of the Medawokantan Sioux Tribe of Wabasha, Minnesota. She went to a convent school at Prairie du Chien, Wisconsin, where she received religious and cultural training and she, too, became a model Christian woman. In 1864, she married Major James McLaughlin and, since she was bilingual, joined him as his official interpreter wherever he was sent. From long hours of talking to and listening to the Indian people, she recorded thirty-seven stories, legends, and myths. The character, Unktomi (Spider), is interwoven throughout many of the stories. Animals are personified and there are mystical occurrences such as ghosts coming back to life. The stories are often humorous. McLaughlin was fifty-two years old when her book of stories was published. Of the writers noted here, she was the oldest and the least educated in a formal sense.

Chief Luther Standing Bear, a Teton Lakota, is the author of *My People the Sioux* (1928, BB 578), *My Indian Boyhood* (1931), *Land of the Spotted Eagle* (1932, BB 655), and *Stories of the Sioux* (1933). Chief Standing Bear's education was obtained at Carlisle Indian School. He later became a schoolteacher on the Rosebud Sioux Reservation in the 1880s. He also joined Buffalo Bill's Wild West Show and traveled abroad extensively. Chief Luther Standing Bear, as a product of the Carlisle Indian School, fell under the same cultural influences as Zitkala-Ša when she taught there at the turn of the century. His book of stories was published at the age of sixty-five.

Ella C. Deloria was also part Yankton. She was born into a very Christian and yet traditional Nakota family. Throughout her life, circumstances aligned themselves in a way that produced the most ideal situation for a scholar.

Foreword

During her early childhood, she remained close to her parents and attended school at St. Elizabeth's at Wakpala, South Dakota, where her father was the presiding presbytor. Here she was in a position to be exposed to the three dialects of the Dakota language. Later she attended All Saints' Episcopal School in Sioux Falls, Oberlin College, and Columbia University. She became a research associate of the anthropologist Franz Boas and spent her entire life collecting and studying the Dakota materials in order to preserve the language, culture, and history of the Sioux.

Ella C. Deloria's *Dakota Texts,* published in 1932 by the American Ethnological Society, is considered to be the most scientific of the written legends. Following the styles of ethnologist James Owen Dorsey and storyteller George Bushotter, Deloria researched and verified at the grassroots level the legends and animal stories that she wrote in the appropriate Sioux dialect. For each story, she entered both a literal and an idiomatic translation into English. In 1979, the English translations of *Dakota Texts* were reprinted by Dakota Press.

It can be seen that Zitkala-Ša led a distinguished line of Sioux writers who had but one goal, and that was to provide the world with information about their people.

IKTOMI AND THE DUCKS

OLD INDIAN LEGENDS

IKTOMI AND THE DUCKS

IKTOMI is a spider fairy. He wears brown deerskin leggins with long soft fringes on either side, and tiny beaded moccasins on his feet. His long black hair is parted in the middle and wrapped with red, red bands. Each round braid hangs over a small brown ear and falls forward over his shoulders.

He even paints his funny face with red and yellow, and draws big black rings around his eyes. He wears a deerskin jacket, with bright colored beads sewed tightly on it. Iktomi dresses like a real Dakota brave. In truth, his paint and deerskins are the best part of him — if ever dress is part of man or fairy.

Iktomi is a wily fellow. His hands are always kept in mischief. He prefers to spread a snare rather than to earn the smallest thing with honest hunting. Why! he laughs outright with wide open mouth when some simple folk are caught in a trap, sure and fast.

He never dreams another lives so bright as he. Often his own conceit leads him hard against the common sense of simpler people.

Poor Iktomi cannot help being a little imp. And so long as he is a naughty fairy, he cannot find a single friend. No one helps him when he is in trouble. No one really loves him. Those who come to admire his handsome beaded jacket and long fringed leggins soon go away sick and tired of his vain, vain words and heartless laughter.

4

Thus Iktomi lives alone in a cone-shaped wigwam upon the plain. One day he sat hungry within his teepee. Suddenly he rushed out, dragging after him his blanket. Quickly spreading it on the ground, he tore up dry tall grass with both his hands and tossed it fast into the blanket.

Tying all the four corners together in a knot, he threw the light bundle of grass over his shoulder.

Snatching up a slender willow stick with his free left hand, he started off with a hop and a leap. From side to side bounced the bundle on his back, as he ran light-footed over the uneven ground. Soon he came to the edge of the great level land. On the hilltop he paused for breath. With wicked smacks of his dry parched lips, as if tasting some tender meat, he looked straight into space toward the marshy river bottom. With a thin palm shading his eyes from the western sun, he peered far away into the lowlands, munching his own cheeks all the while. "Ah-ha!" grunted he, satisfied with what he saw.

A group of wild ducks were dancing and feasting in the marshes. With wings outspread, tip to tip, they moved up and down in a large circle. Within the ring, around a small drum, sat the chosen singers, nodding their heads and blinking their eyes.

They sang in unison a merry dance-song, and beat a lively tattoo on the drum.

Following a winding footpath near by, came a bent figure of a Dakota brave. He bore on his back a very large bundle. With a willow cane he propped himself up as he staggered along beneath his burden.

"Ho! who is there?" called out a curious old duck, still bobbing up and down in the circular dance.

Hereupon the drummers stretched their necks till they strangled their song for a look at the stranger passing by.

"Ho, Iktomi! Old fellow, pray tell us what you carry in your blanket. Do not hurry off! Stop! halt!" urged one of the singers.

"Stop! stay! Show us what is in your blanket!" cried out other voices.

"My friends, I must not spoil your dance. Oh, you would not care to see if you only knew what is in my blanket. Sing on! dance on! I must not show you what I carry on my back," answered Iktomi, nudging his own sides with his elbows. This reply broke up the ring entirely. Now all the ducks crowded about Iktomi.

"We must see what you carry! We must know what is in your blanket!" they shouted in both his ears. Some even brushed their wings against the mysterious bundle. Nudging himself again, wily Iktomi said, "My friends, 't is only a pack of songs I carry in my blanket."

7

"Oh, then let us hear your songs!" cried the curious ducks.

At length Iktomi consented to sing his songs. With delight all the ducks flapped their wings and cried together, "Hoye! hoye!"

Iktomi, with great care, laid down his bundle on the ground.

"I will build first a round straw house, for I never sing my songs in the open air," said he.

Quickly he bent green willow sticks, planting both ends of each pole into the earth. These he covered thick with reeds and grasses. Soon the straw hut was ready. One by one the fat ducks waddled in through a small opening, which was the only entrance way. Beside the door Iktomi stood smiling, as the ducks, eyeing his bundle of songs, strutted into the hut.

In a strange low voice Iktomi began his queer old tunes. All the ducks sat round-eyed in a circle about the mysterious singer. It was dim in that straw hut, for Iktomi had not forgot to cover up the small entrance way. All of a sudden his song burst into full voice. As the startled ducks sat uneasily on the ground, Iktomi changed his tune into a minor strain. These were the words he sang:

"Ištokmus wacipo, tuwayatunwanpi kinhan išta nišašapi kta," which is, "With eyes closed you must dance. He who dares to open his eyes, forever red eyes shall have."

Up rose the circle of seated ducks and holding their wings close against their sides began to dance to the rhythm of Iktomi's song and drum.

With eyes closed they did dance! Iktomi ceased to beat his drum. He began to sing louder and faster. He seemed to be moving about in the center of the ring. No duck dared blink a wink. Each one shut his eyes very tight and danced even harder.

9

Up and down! Shifting to the right of them they hopped round and round in that blind dance. It was a difficult dance for the curious folk.

At length one of the dancers could close his eyes no longer! It was a Skiska who peeped the least tiny blink at Iktomi within the center of the circle. "Oh! oh!" squawked he in awful terror! "Run! fly! Iktomi is twisting your heads and breaking your necks! Run out and fly! fly!" he cried. Hereupon the ducks opened their eyes. There beside Iktomi's bundle of songs lay half of their crowd—flat on their backs.

Out they flew through the opening Skiska had made as he rushed forth with his alarm.

But as they soared high into the blue sky they cried to one another: "Oh! your eyes are red-red!" "And yours are red-red!" For the warning words of the magic minor strain had proven true. "Ah-ha!" laughed Iktomi, untying the four corners of his

10

blanket, "I shall sit no more hungry within my dwelling." Homeward he trudged along with nice fat ducks in his blanket. He left the little straw hut for the rains and winds to pull down.

Having reached his own teepee on the high level lands, Iktomi kindled a large fire out of doors. He planted sharp-pointed sticks around the leaping flames. On each stake he fastened a duck to roast. A few he buried under the ashes to bake. Disappearing within his teepee, he came out again with some huge seashells. These were his dishes. Placing one under each roasting duck, he muttered, "The sweet fat oozing out will taste well with the hard-cooked breasts."

Heaping more willows upon the fire, Iktomi sat down on the ground with crossed shins. A long chin between his knees pointed toward the red flames, while his eyes were on the browning ducks.

Just above his ankles he clasped and unclasped his long bony fingers. Now and then he sniffed impatiently the savory odor.

The brisk wind which stirred the fire also played with a squeaky old tree beside Iktomi's wigwam.

From side to side the tree was swaying and crying in an old man's voice, "Help! I'll break! I'll fall!" Iktomi shrugged his great shoulders, but did not once take his eyes from the ducks. The dripping of amber oil into pearly dishes, drop by drop, pleased his hungry eyes. Still the old tree man called for help. "Hĕ! What sound is it that makes my ear ache!" exclaimed Iktomi, holding a hand on his ear.

He rose and looked around. The squeaking came from the tree. Then he began climbing the tree to find the disagreeable sound. He placed his foot right on a cracked limb without seeing it. Just then a whiff of wind came rushing by and pressed together the broken edges. There in a strong wooden hand Iktomi's foot was caught.

"Oh! my foot is crushed!" he howled like a coward. In vain he pulled and puffed to free himself.

While sitting a prisoner on the tree he spied, through his tears, a pack of gray wolves roaming over the level lands. Waving his hands toward them, he called in his loudest voice, " Hĕ! Gray wolves! Don't you come here! I'm caught fast in the tree so that my duck feast is getting cold. Don't you come to eat up my meal."

The leader of the pack upon hearing Iktomi's words turned to his comrades and said:

"Ah! hear the foolish fellow! He says he has a duck feast to be eaten! Let us hurry there for our share!" Away bounded the wolves toward Iktomi's lodge.

From the tree Iktomi watched the hungry

13

wolves eat up his nicely browned fat ducks.
His foot pained him more and more. He
heard them crack the small round bones
with their strong long teeth and eat out
the oily marrow. Now severe pains shot
up from his foot through his whole body.
"Hin-hin-hin!" sobbed Iktomi. Real tears
washed brown streaks across his red-painted
cheeks. Smacking their lips, the wolves
began to leave the place, when Iktomi cried
out like a pouting child, "At least you have
left my baking under the ashes!"

"Ho! po!" shouted the mischievous
wolves; "he says more ducks are to be
found under the ashes! Come! Let us
have our fill this once!"

Running back to the dead fire, they
pawed out the ducks with such rude haste
that a cloud of ashes rose like gray smoke
over them.

"Hin-hin-hin!" moaned Iktomi, when
the wolves had scampered off. All too late,

14

the sturdy breeze returned, and, passing by, pulled apart the broken edges of the tree. Iktomi was released. But alas! he had no duck feast.

IKTOMI'S BLANKET

IKTOMI'S BLANKET

Alone within his teepee sat Iktomi. The sun was but a hand's-breadth from the western edge of land.

"Those bad, bad gray wolves! They ate up all my nice fat ducks!" muttered he, rocking his body to and fro.

He was cuddling the evil memory he bore those hungry wolves. At last he ceased to sway his body backward and forward, but sat still and stiff as a stone image.

"Oh! I'll go to Inyan, the great-grandfather, and pray for food!" he exclaimed.

At once he hurried forth from his teepee and, with his blanket over one shoulder, drew nigh to a huge rock on a hillside.

With half-crouching, half-running strides, he fell upon Inyan with outspread hands.

"Grandfather! pity me. I am hungry. I am starving. Give me food. Great-grandfather, give me meat to eat!" he cried. All the while he stroked and caressed the face of the great stone god.

The all-powerful Great Spirit, who makes the trees and grass, can hear the voice of those who pray in many varied ways. The hearing of Inyan, the large hard stone, was the one most sought after. He was the great-grandfather, for he had sat upon the hillside many, many seasons. He had seen the prairie put on a snow-white blanket and then change it for a bright green robe more than a thousand times.

Still unaffected by the myriad moons he rested on the everlasting hill, listening to the prayers of Indian warriors. Before the finding of the magic arrow he had sat there.

Now, as Iktomi prayed and wept before the great-grandfather, the sky in the west was red like a glowing face. The sunset poured a soft mellow light upon the huge gray stone and the solitary figure beside it. It was the smile of the Great Spirit upon the grandfather and the wayward child.

The prayer was heard. Iktomi knew it. "Now, grandfather, accept my offering; 't is all I have," said Iktomi as he spread his half-worn blanket upon Inyan's cold shoulders. Then Iktomi, happy with the smile of the sunset sky, followed a footpath leading toward a thicketed ravine. He had not gone many paces into the shrubbery when before him lay a freshly wounded deer!

"This is the answer from the red western sky!" cried Iktomi with hands uplifted.

Slipping a long thin blade from out his belt, he cut large chunks of choice meat. Sharpening some willow sticks, he planted them around a wood-pile he had ready to kindle. On these stakes he meant to roast the venison.

While he was rubbing briskly two long sticks to start a fire, the sun in the west fell out of the sky below the edge of land. Twilight was over all. Iktomi felt the cold night air upon his bare neck and shoulders. "Ough!" he shivered as he wiped his knife on the grass. Tucking it in a beaded case hanging from his belt, Iktomi stood erect, looking about. He shivered again. "Ough! Ah! I am cold. I wish I had my blanket!" whispered he, hovering over the pile of dry sticks and the sharp stakes round about it. Suddenly he paused and dropped his hands at his sides.

"The old great-grandfather does not feel the cold as I do. He does not need my old blanket as I do. I wish I had not given it to him. Oh! I think I'll run up there and take it back!" said he, pointing his long chin toward the large gray stone.

Iktomi, in the warm sunshine, had no need of his blanket, and it had been very easy to part with a thing which he could not miss. But the chilly night wind quite froze his ardent thank-offering.

Thus running up the hillside, his teeth chattering all the way, he drew near to Inyan, the sacred symbol. Seizing one corner of the half-worn blanket, Iktomi pulled it off with a jerk.

"Give my blanket back, old grandfather! You do not need it. I do!" This was very wrong, yet Iktomi did it, for his wit was not wisdom. Drawing the blanket tight over his shoulders, he descended the hill with hurrying feet.

He was soon upon the edge of the ravine. A young moon, like a bright bent bow, climbed up from the southwest horizon a little way into the sky.

In this pale light Iktomi stood motionless as a ghost amid the thicket. His wood-

23

pile was not yet kindled. His pointed stakes were still bare as he had left them. But where was the deer — the venison he had felt warm in his hands a moment ago? It was gone. Only the dry rib bones lay on the ground like giant fingers from an open grave. Iktomi was troubled. At length, stooping over the white dried bones, he took hold of one and shook it. The bones, loose in their sockets, rattled together at his touch. Iktomi let go his hold. He sprang back amazed. And though he wore a blanket his teeth chattered more than ever. Then his blunted sense will surprise you, little reader; for instead of being grieved that he had taken back his blanket, he cried aloud, "Hin-hin-hin! If only I had eaten the venison before going for my blanket!"

Those tears no longer moved the hand of the Generous Giver. They were selfish tears. The Great Spirit does not heed them ever.

IKTOMI AND THE MUSKRAT

IKTOMI AND THE MUSKRAT

BESIDE a white lake, beneath a large grown willow tree, sat Iktomi on the bare ground. The heap of smouldering ashes told of a recent open fire. With ankles crossed together around a pot of soup, Iktomi bent over some delicious boiled fish.

Fast he dipped his black horn spoon into the soup, for he was ravenous. Iktomi had no regular meal times. Often when he was hungry he went without food.

Well hid between the lake and the wild rice, he looked nowhere save into the pot of fish. Not knowing when the next meal would be, he meant to eat enough now to last some time.

"How, how, my friend!" said a voice out of the wild rice. Iktomi started. He almost choked with his soup. He peered through the long reeds from where he sat with his long horn spoon in mid-air.

"How, my friend!" said the voice again, this time close at his side. Iktomi turned and there stood a dripping muskrat who had just come out of the lake.

"Oh, it is my friend who startled me. I wondered if among the wild rice some spirit voice was talking. How, how, my friend!" said Iktomi. The muskrat stood smiling. On his lips hung a ready "Yes, my friend," when Iktomi would ask, "My friend, will you sit down beside me and share my food?"

That was the custom of the plains people. Yet Iktomi sat silent. He hummed an old dance-song and beat gently on the edge of the pot with his buffalo-horn spoon. The muskrat began to feel awkward before such lack of hospitality and wished himself under water.

Iktomi and the Muskrat

After many heart throbs Iktomi stopped drumming with his horn ladle, and looking upward into the muskrat's face, he said:

"My friend, let us run a race to see who shall win this pot of fish. If I win, I shall not need to share it with you. If you win, you shall have half of it." Springing to his feet, Iktomi began at once to tighten the belt about his waist.

"My friend Ikto, I cannot run a race with you! I am not a swift runner, and you are nimble as a deer. We shall not run any race together," answered the hungry muskrat.

For a moment Iktomi stood with a hand on his long protruding chin. His eyes were fixed upon something in the air. The muskrat looked out of the corners of his eyes without moving his head. He watched the wily Iktomi concocting a plot.

"Yes, yes," said Iktomi, suddenly turning his gaze upon the unwelcome visitor;

"I shall carry a large stone on my back. That will slacken my usual speed; and the race will be a fair one."

Saying this he laid a firm hand upon the muskrat's shoulder and started off along the edge of the lake. When they reached the opposite side Iktomi pried about in search of a heavy stone.

He found one half-buried in the shallow water. Pulling it out upon dry land, he wrapped it in his blanket.

"Now, my friend, you shall run on the left side of the lake, I on the other. The race is for the boiled fish in yonder kettle!" said Iktomi.

The muskrat helped to lift the heavy stone upon Iktomi's back. Then they parted. Each took a narrow path through the tall reeds fringing the shore. Iktomi found his load a heavy one. Perspiration hung like beads on his brow. His chest heaved hard and fast.

Iktomi and the Muskrat

He looked across the lake to see how far the muskrat had gone, but nowhere did he see any sign of him. " Well, he is running low under the wild rice!" said he. Yet as he scanned the tall grasses on the lake shore, he saw not one stir as if to make way for the runner. "Ah, has he gone so fast ahead that the disturbed grasses in his trail have quieted again?" exclaimed Iktomi. With that thought he quickly dropped the heavy stone. " No more of this!" said he, patting his chest with both hands.

Off with a springing bound, he ran swiftly toward the goal. Tufts of reeds and grass fell flat under his feet. Hardly had they raised their heads when Iktomi was many paces gone.

Soon he reached the heap of cold ashes. Iktomi halted stiff as if he had struck an invisible cliff. His black eyes showed a ring of white about them as he stared at the empty ground. There was no pot of boiled fish! There was no water-man in sight! "Oh, if only I had shared my food like a real Dakota, I would not have lost it all! Why did I not know the muskrat would run through the water? He swims faster than I could ever run! That is what he has done. He has laughed at me for carrying a weight on my back while he shot hither like an arrow!"

Crying thus to himself, Iktomi stepped to the water's brink. He stooped forward with a hand on each bent knee and peeped far into the deep water.

"There!" he exclaimed, "I see you, my friend, sitting with your ankles wound around my little pot of fish! My friend, I am hungry. Give me a bone!"

"Ha! ha! ha!" laughed the water-man, the muskrat. The sound did not rise up out of the lake, for it came down from overhead. With his hands still on his knees, Iktomi turned his face upward into the great willow tree.   Opening wide his mouth he begged, " My friend, my friend, give me a bone to gnaw ! "

" Ha ! ha ! " laughed the muskrat, and leaning over the limb he sat upon, he let fall a small sharp bone which dropped right into Iktomi's throat.   Iktomi almost choked to death before he could get it out.   In the tree the muskrat sat laughing loud.   " Next time, say to a visiting friend, ' Be seated beside me, my friend.   Let me share with you my food.' "

IKTOMI AND THE COYOTE

IKTOMI AND THE COYOTE

AFAR off upon a large level land, a summer sun was shining bright. Here and there over the rolling green were tall bunches of coarse gray weeds. Iktomi in his fringed buckskins walked alone across the prairie with a black bare head glossy in the sunlight. He walked through the grass without following any well-worn footpath.

From one large bunch of coarse weeds to another he wound his way about the great plain. He lifted his foot lightly and placed it gently forward like a wildcat prowling noiselessly through the thick grass. He stopped a few steps away from a very large bunch of wild sage. From shoulder to shoulder he tilted his head. Still farther he bent from side to side, first low over one hip and then over the other. Far forward he stooped, stretching his long thin neck like a duck, to see what lay under a fur coat beyond the bunch of coarse grass.

A sleek gray-faced prairie wolf! his pointed black nose tucked in between his four feet drawn snugly together; his handsome bushy tail wound over his nose and feet; a coyote fast asleep in the shadow of a bunch of grass! — this is what Iktomi spied. Carefully he raised one foot and cautiously reached out with his toes. Gently, gently he lifted the foot behind and placed it before the other. Thus he came nearer and nearer to the round fur ball lying motionless under the sage grass.

Now Iktomi stood beside it, looking at the closed eyelids that did not quiver the least bit. Pressing his lips into straight lines and nodding his head slowly, he bent over the wolf. He held his ear close to the coyote's nose, but not a breath of air stirred from it.

"Dead!" said he at last. "Dead, but not long since he ran over these plains! See! there in his paw is caught a fresh feather. He is nice fat meat!" Taking hold of the paw with the bird feather fast on it, he exclaimed, "Why, he is still warm! I'll carry him to my dwelling and have a roast for my evening meal. Ah-ha!" he laughed, as he seized the coyote by its two fore paws and its two hind feet and swung him over head across his shoulders. The wolf was large and the teepee was far across the prairie. Iktomi trudged along with his burden, smacking his hungry lips together. He blinked his eyes hard to keep out the salty perspiration streaming down his face.

All the while the coyote on his back lay gazing into the sky with wide open eyes. His long white teeth fairly gleamed as he smiled and smiled.

"To ride on one's own feet is tiresome, but to be carried like a warrior from a brave fight is great fun!" said the coyote in his heart. He had never been borne on any one's back before and the new experience delighted him. He lay there lazily on Iktomi's shoulders, now and then blinking blue winks. Did you never see a birdie blink a blue wink? This is how it first became a saying among the plains people. When a bird stands aloof watching your strange ways, a thin bluish white tissue slips quickly over his eyes and as quickly off again; so quick that you think it was only a mysterious blue wink. Sometimes when children grow drowsy they blink blue winks, while others who are too proud to look with friendly eyes upon people blink in this cold bird-manner.

The coyote was affected by both sleepiness and pride. His winks were almost as blue as the sky. In the midst of his

new pleasure the swaying motion ceased.
Iktomi had reached his dwelling place. The
coyote felt drowsy no longer, for in the next
instant he was slipping out of Iktomi's
hands. He was falling, falling through
space, and then he struck the ground with
such a bump he did not wish to breathe for
a while. He wondered what Iktomi would
do, thus he lay still where he fell. Hum-
ming a dance-song, one from his bundle of
mystery songs, Iktomi hopped and darted
about at an imaginary dance and feast.
He gathered dry willow sticks and broke
them in two against his knee. He built a
large fire out of doors. The flames leaped
up high in red and yellow streaks. Now
Iktomi returned to the coyote who had been
looking on through his eyelashes.

Taking him again by his paws and hind
feet, he swung him to and fro. Then as
the wolf swung toward the red flames,
Iktomi let him go. Once again the coyote

fell through space. Hot air smote his nostrils. He saw red dancing fire, and now he struck a bed of cracking embers. With a quick turn he leaped out of the flames. From his heels were scattered a shower of red coals upon Iktomi's bare arms and shoulders. Dumfounded, Iktomi thought he saw a spirit walk out of his fire. His jaws fell apart. He thrust a palm to his face, hard over his mouth! He could scarce keep from shrieking.

Rolling over and over on the grass and rubbing the sides of his head against the ground, the coyote soon put out the fire on his fur. Iktomi's eyes were almost ready to jump out of his head as he stood cooling a burn on his brown arm with his breath.

Sitting on his haunches, on the opposite side of the fire from where Iktomi stood, the coyote began to laugh at him.

"Another day, my friend, do not take too much for granted. Make sure the enemy is stone dead before you make a fire!"

Then off he ran so swiftly that his long bushy tail hung out in a straight line with his back.

IKTOMI AND THE FAWN

IKTOMI AND THE FAWN

In one of his wanderings through the wooded lands, Iktomi saw a rare bird sitting high in a tree-top. Its long fan-like tail feathers had caught all the beautiful colors of the rainbow. Handsome in the glistening summer sun sat the bird of rainbow plumage. Iktomi hurried hither with his eyes fast on the bird.

He stood beneath the tree looking long and wistfully at the peacock's bright feathers. At length he heaved a sigh and began: "Oh, I wish I had such pretty feathers! How I wish I were not I! If only I were a handsome feathered creature how happy I would be! I'd be so glad to sit upon a very high tree and bask in the summer sun like you!" said he suddenly, pointing his bony finger up toward the peacock, who was eyeing the stranger below, turning his head from side to side.

"I beg of you make me into a bird with green and purple feathers like yours!" implored Iktomi, tired now of playing the brave in beaded buckskins. The peacock then spoke to Iktomi: "I have a magic power. My touch will change you in a moment into the most beautiful peacock if you can keep one condition."

"Yes! yes!" shouted Iktomi, jumping up and down, patting his lips with his palm, which caused his voice to vibrate in a peculiar fashion. "Yes! yes! I could keep ten conditions if only you would change me into a bird with long, bright tail feathers. Oh, I am so ugly! I am so tired of being myself! Change me! Do!"

Hereupon the peacock spread out both his wings, and scarce moving them, he sailed slowly down upon the ground. Right beside

Iktomi he alighted. Very low in Iktomi's ear the peacock whispered, "Are you willing to keep one condition, though hard it be?"

"Yes! yes! I've told you ten of them if need be!" exclaimed Iktomi, with some impatience.

"Then I pronounce you a handsome feathered bird. No longer are you Iktomi the mischief-maker." Saying this the peacock touched Iktomi with the tips of his wings.

Iktomi vanished at the touch. There stood beneath the tree two handsome peacocks. While one of the pair strutted about with a head turned aside as if dazzled by his own bright-tinted tail feathers, the other bird soared slowly upward. He sat quiet and unconscious of his gay plumage. He seemed content to perch there on a large limb in the warm sunshine.

After a little while the vain peacock, dizzy with his bright colors, spread out his wings and lit on the same branch with the elder bird.

"Oh!" he exclaimed, "how hard to fly! Brightly tinted feathers are handsome, but I wish they were light enough to fly!" Just there the elder bird interrupted him. "That is the one condition. Never try to fly like other birds. Upon the day you try to fly you shall be changed into your former self."

"Oh, what a shame that bright feathers cannot fly into the sky!" cried the peacock. Already he grew restless. He longed to soar through space. He yearned to fly above the trees high upward to the sun.

"Oh, there I see a flock of birds flying thither! Oh! oh!" said he, flapping his wings, "I must try my wings! I am tired of bright tail feathers. I want to try my wings."

"No, no!" clucked the elder bird. The flock of chattering birds flew by with

whirring wings. "O͞op! o͞op!" called some
to their mates.

Possessed by an irrepressible impulse the
Iktomi peacock called out, "Hĕ! I want
to come! Wait for me!" and with that he
gave a lunge into the air. The flock of
flying feathers wheeled about and lowered
over the tree whence came the peacock's
cry. Only one rare bird sat on the tree,
and beneath, on the ground, stood a brave
in brown buckskins.

"I am my old self again!" groaned
Iktomi in a sad voice. "Make me over,
pretty bird. Try me this once again!"
he pleaded in vain.

"Old Iktomi wants to fly! Ah! We
cannot wait for him!" sang the birds as
they flew away.

Muttering unhappy vows to himself, Iktomi had not gone far when he chanced
upon a bunch of long slender arrows. One
by one they rose in the air and shot a

straight line over the prairie. Others shot
up into the blue sky and were soon lost to
sight. Only one was left. He was making ready for his flight when Iktomi rushed
upon him and wailed, "I want to be an
arrow! Make me into an arrow! I want
to pierce the blue Blue overhead. I want
to strike yonder summer sun in its center.
Make me into an arrow!"

"Can you keep a condition? One condition, though hard it be?" the arrow
turned to ask.

"Yes! yes!" shouted Iktomi, delighted.

Hereupon the slender arrow tapped him
gently with his sharp flint beak. There
was no Iktomi, but two arrows stood ready
to fly. "Now, young arrow, this is the
one condition. Your flight must always
be in a straight line. Never turn a curve
nor jump about like a young fawn," said
the arrow magician. He spoke slowly and
sternly.

At once he set about to teach the new arrow how to shoot in a long straight line.

"This is the way to pierce the Blue overhead," said he; and off he spun high into the sky.

While he was gone a herd of deer came trotting by. Behind them played the young fawns together. They frolicked about like kittens. They bounced on all fours like balls. Then they pitched forward, kicking their heels in the air. The Iktomi arrow watched them so happy on the ground. Looking quickly up into the sky, he said in his heart, "The magician is out of sight. I'll just romp and frolic with these fawns until he returns. Fawns! Friends, do not fear me. I want to jump and leap with you. I long to be happy as you are," said he. The young fawns stopped with stiff legs and stared at the speaking arrow with large brown wondering eyes. "See!

I can jump as well as you!" went on Iktomi. He gave one tiny leap like a fawn. All of a sudden the fawns snorted with extended nostrils at what they beheld. There among them stood Iktomi in brown buckskins, and the strange talking arrow was gone.

"Oh! I am myself. My old self!" cried Iktomi, pinching himself and plucking imaginary pieces out of his jacket.

"Hin-hin-hin! I wanted to fly!"

The real arrow now returned to the earth. He alighted very near Iktomi. From the high sky he had seen the fawns playing on the green. He had seen Iktomi make his one leap, and the charm was broken. Iktomi became his former self.

"Arrow, my friend, change me once more!" begged Iktomi.

"No, no more," replied the arrow. Then away he shot through the air in the direction his comrades had flown.

By this time the fawns gathered close around Iktomi. They poked their noses at him trying to know who he was.

Iktomi's tears were like a spring shower. A new desire dried them quickly away. Stepping boldly to the largest fawn, he looked closely at the little brown spots all over the furry face.

"Oh, fawn! What beautiful brown spots on your face! Fawn, dear little fawn, can you tell me how those brown spots were made on your face?"

"Yes," said the fawn. "When I was very, very small, my mother marked them on my face with a red hot fire. She dug a large hole in the ground and made a soft bed of grass and twigs in it. Then she placed me gently there. She covered me over with dry sweet grass and piled dry cedars on top. From a neighbor's fire she brought hither a red, red ember. This she tucked carefully in at my head. This is how the brown spots were made on my face."

"Now, fawn, my friend, will you do the same for me? Won't you mark my face with brown, brown spots just like yours?" asked Iktomi, always eager to be like other people.

"Yes. I can dig the ground and fill it with dry grass and sticks. If you will jump into the pit, I'll cover you with sweet smelling grass and cedar wood," answered the fawn.

"Say," interrupted Ikto, "will you be sure to cover me with a great deal of dry grass and twigs? You will make sure that the spots will be as brown as those you wear."

"Oh, yes. I'll pile up grass and willows once oftener than my mother did."

"Now let us dig the hole, pull the grass, and gather sticks," cried Iktomi in glee.

Thus with his own hands he aids in making his grave. After the hole was dug and cushioned with grass, Iktomi, muttering something about brown spots, leaped down into it. Lengthwise, flat on his back, he lay. While the fawn covered him over with cedars, a far-away voice came up through them, "Brown, brown spots to wear forever!" A red ember was tucked under the dry grass. Off scampered the fawns after their mothers; and when a great distance away they looked backward. They saw a blue smoke rising, writhing upward till it vanished in the blue ether.

"Is that Iktomi's spirit?" asked one fawn of another.

"No! I think he would jump out before he could burn into smoke and cinders," answered his comrade.

THE BADGER AND THE BEAR

THE BADGER AND THE BEAR

On the edge of a forest there lived a large family of badgers. In the ground their dwelling was made. Its walls and roof were covered with rocks and straw.

Old father badger was a great hunter. He knew well how to track the deer and buffalo. Every day he came home carrying on his back some wild game. This kept mother badger very busy, and the baby badgers very chubby. While the well-fed children played about, digging little make-believe dwellings, their mother hung thin sliced meats upon long willow racks. As fast as the meats were dried and seasoned by sun and wind, she packed them carefully away in a large thick bag.

This bag was like a huge stiff envelope, but far more beautiful to see, for it was painted all over with many bright colors. These firmly tied bags of dried meat were laid upon the rocks in the walls of the dwelling. In this way they were both useful and decorative.

One day father badger did not go off for a hunt. He stayed at home, making new arrows. His children sat about him on the ground floor. Their small black eyes danced with delight as they watched the gay colors painted upon the arrows.

All of a sudden there was heard a heavy footfall near the entrance way. The oval-shaped door-frame was pushed aside. In stepped a large black foot with great big claws. Then the other clumsy foot came next. All the while the baby badgers stared hard at the unexpected comer. After the second foot, in peeped the head of a big black bear! His black nose was dry and parched. Silently he entered the dwelling and sat down on the ground by the doorway.

His black eyes never left the painted bags
on the rocky walls. He guessed what was
in them. He was a very hungry bear. Seeing the racks of red meat hanging in the
yard, he had come to visit the badger family.

Though he was a stranger and his strong
paws and jaws frightened the small badgers,
the father said, "How, how, friend! Your
lips and nose look feverish and hungry.
Will you eat with us?"

"Yes, my friend," said the bear. "I am
starved. I saw your racks of red fresh meat,
and knowing your heart is kind, I came
hither. Give me meat to eat, my friend."

Hereupon the mother badger took long
strides across the room, and as she had to
pass in front of the strange visitor, she
said: "Ah han! Allow me to pass!" which
was an apology.

"How, how!" replied the bear, drawing
himself closer to the wall and crossing his
shins together.

Mother badger chose the most tender red meat, and soon over a bed of coals she broiled the venison.

That day the bear had all he could eat. At nightfall he rose, and smacking his lips together,—that is the noisy way of saying "the food was very good!"—he left the badger dwelling. The baby badgers, peeping through the door-flap after the shaggy bear, saw him disappear into the woods near by.

Day after day the crackling of twigs in the forest told of heavy footsteps. Out would come the same black bear. He never lifted the door-flap, but thrusting it aside entered slowly in. Always in the same place by the entrance way he sat down with crossed shins.

His daily visits were so regular that mother badger placed a fur rug in his place. She did not wish a guest in her dwelling to sit upon the bare hard ground.

The Badger and the Bear

At last one time when the bear returned, his nose was bright and black. His coat was glossy. He had grown fat upon the badger's hospitality.

As he entered the dwelling a pair of wicked gleams shot out of his shaggy head. Surprised by the strange behavior of the guest who remained standing upon the rug, leaning his round back against the wall, father badger queried: "How, my friend! What?"

The bear took one stride forward and shook his paw in the badger's face. He said: "I am strong, very strong!"

"Yes, yes, so you are," replied the badger. From the farther end of the room mother badger muttered over her bead work: "Yes, you grew strong from our well-filled bowls."

The bear smiled, showing a row of large sharp teeth.

"I have no dwelling. I have no bags of

dried meat. I have no arrows. All these
I have found here on this spot," said he,
stamping his heavy foot. "I want them!
See! I am strong!" repeated he, lifting
both his terrible paws.

Quietly the father badger spoke: "I fed
you. I called you friend, though you came
here a stranger and a beggar. For the
sake of my little ones leave us in peace."

Mother badger, in her excited way, had
pierced hard through the buckskin and stuck
her fingers repeatedly with her sharp awl
until she had laid aside her work. Now,
while her husband was talking to the bear,
she motioned with her hands to the children.
On tiptoe they hastened to her side.

For reply came a low growl. It grew
louder and more fierce. "Wä-ough!" he
roared, and by force hurled the badgers
out. First the father badger; then the
mother. The little badgers he tossed by
pairs. He threw them hard upon the

ground. Standing in the entrance way and showing his ugly teeth, he snarled, "Be gone!"

The father and mother badger, having gained their feet, picked up their kicking little babes, and, wailing aloud, drew the air into their flattened lungs till they could stand alone upon their feet. No sooner had the baby badgers caught their breath than they howled and shrieked with pain and fright. Ah! what a dismal cry was theirs as the whole badger family went forth wailing from out their own dwelling! A little distance away from their stolen house the father badger built a small round hut. He made it of bent willows and covered it with dry grass and twigs.

This was shelter for the night; but alas! it was empty of food and arrows. All day father badger prowled through the forest, but without his arrows he could not get food for his children. Upon his return, the cry of the little ones for meat, the sad quiet of the mother with bowed head, hurt him like a poisoned arrow wound.

" I 'll beg meat for you!" said he in an unsteady voice. Covering his head and entire body in a long loose robe he halted beside the big black bear. The bear was slicing red meat to hang upon the rack. He did not pause for a look at the comer. As the badger stood there unrecognized, he saw that the bear had brought with him his whole family. Little cubs played under the high-hanging new meats. They laughed and pointed with their wee noses upward at the thin sliced meats upon the poles.

" Have you no heart, Black Bear? My children are starving. Give me a small piece of meat for them," begged the badger.

" Wä-ough!" growled the angry bear, and pounced upon the badger. " Be gone!" said he, and with his big hind foot he sent father badger sprawling on the ground.

68

The Badger and the Bear

All the little ruffian bears hooted and shouted "ha-ha!" to see the beggar fall upon his face. There was one, however, who did not even smile. He was the youngest cub. His fur coat was not as black and glossy as those his elders wore. The hair was dry and dingy. It looked much more like kinky wool. He was the ugly cub. Poor little baby bear! he had always been laughed at by his older brothers. He could not help being himself. He could not change the differences between himself and his brothers. Thus again, though the rest laughed aloud at the badger's fall, he did not see the joke. His face was long and earnest. In his heart he was sad to see the badgers crying and starving. In his breast spread a burning desire to share his food with them.

"I shall not ask my father for meat to give away. He would say 'No!' Then my brothers would laugh at me," said the ugly baby bear to himself.

In an instant, as if his good intention had passed from him, he was singing happily and skipping around his father at work. Singing in his small high voice and dragging his feet in long strides after him, as if a prankish spirit oozed out from his heels, he strayed off through the tall grass. He was ambling toward the small round hut. When directly in front of the entrance way, he made a quick side kick with his left hind leg. Lo! there fell into the badger's hut a piece of fresh meat. It was tough meat, full of sinews, yet it was the only piece he could take without his father's notice.

Thus having given meat to the hungry badgers, the ugly baby bear ran quickly away to his father again.

On the following day the father badger came back once more. He stood watching the big bear cutting thin slices of meat.

" Give — " he began, when the bear turning upon him with a growl, thrust him

cruelly aside. The badger fell on his hands.
He fell where the grass was wet with the
blood of the newly carved buffalo. His
keen starving eyes caught sight of a little
red clot lying bright upon the green. Looking fearfully toward the bear and seeing his
head was turned away, he snatched up the
small thick blood. Underneath his girdled
blanket he hid it in his hand.

On his return to his family, he said
within himself: "I'll pray the Great Spirit
to bless it." Thus he built a small round
lodge. Sprinkling water upon the heated
heap of sacred stones within, he made ready
to purge his body. "The buffalo blood,
too, must be purified before I ask a blessing
upon it," thought the badger. He carried
it into the sacred vapor lodge. After placing it near the sacred stones, he sat down
beside it. After a long silence, he muttered: "Great Spirit, bless this little buffalo
blood." Then he arose, and with a quiet

dignity stepped out of the lodge. Close behind him some one followed. The badger turned to look over his shoulder and to his great joy he beheld a Dakota brave in handsome buckskins. In his hand he carried a magic arrow. Across his back dangled a long fringed quiver. In answer to the badger's prayer, the avenger had sprung from out the red globules.

"My son!" exclaimed the badger with extended right hand.

"How, father," replied the brave; "I am your avenger!"

Immediately the badger told the sad story of his hungry little ones and the stingy bear.

Listening closely the young man stood looking steadily upon the ground.

At length the father badger moved away.

"Where?" queried the avenger.

"My son, we have no food. I am going again to beg for meat," answered the badger.

"Then I go with you," replied the young brave. This made the old badger happy. He was proud of his son. He was delighted to be called "father" by the first human creature.

The bear saw the badger coming in the distance. He narrowed his eyes at the tall stranger walking beside him. He spied the arrow. At once he guessed it was the avenger of whom he had heard long, long ago. As they approached, the bear stood erect with a hand on his thigh. He smiled upon them.

"How, badger, my friend! Here is my knife. Cut your favorite pieces from the deer," said he, holding out a long thin blade.

"How!" said the badger eagerly. He wondered what had inspired the big bear to such a generous deed. The young avenger waited till the badger took the long knife in his hand.

Gazing full into the black bear's face, he said: "I come to do justice. You have returned only a knife to my poor father. Now return to him his dwelling." His voice was deep and powerful. In his black eyes burned a steady fire.

The long strong teeth of the bear rattled against each other, and his shaggy body shook with fear. "Ahōw!" cried he, as if he had been shot. Running into the dwelling he gasped, breathless and trembling, "Come out, all of you! This is the badger's dwelling. We must flee to the forest for fear of the avenger who carries the magic arrow."

Out they hurried, all the bears, and disappeared into the woods.

Singing and laughing, the badgers returned to their own dwelling.

Then the avenger left them.

"I go," said he in parting, "over the earth."

THE TREE-BOUND

THE TREE–BOUND

It was a clear summer day. The blue, blue sky dropped low over the edge of the green level land. A large yellow sun hung directly overhead.

The singing of birds filled the summer space between earth and sky with sweet music. Again and again sang a yellow-breasted birdie —"Koda Ni Dakota!" He insisted upon it. "Koda Ni Dakota!" which was "Friend, you're a Dakota! Friend, you're a Dakota!" Perchance the birdie meant the avenger with the magic arrow, for there across the plain he strode. He was handsome in his paint and feathers, proud with his great buckskin quiver on his back and a long bow in his hand. Afar to an eastern camp of cone-shaped teepees he was going. There over the Indian village hovered a large red eagle threatening the safety of the people. Every morning rose this terrible red bird out of a high chalk bluff and spreading out his gigantic wings soared slowly over the round camp ground. Then it was that the people, terror-stricken, ran screaming into their lodges. Covering their heads with their blankets, they sat trembling with fear. No one dared to venture out till the red eagle had disappeared beyond the west, where meet the blue and green.

In vain tried the chieftain of the tribe to find among his warriors a powerful marksman who could send a death arrow to the man-hungry bird. At last to urge his men to their utmost skill he bade his crier proclaim a new reward.

Of the chieftain's two beautiful daughters he would have his choice who brought the dreaded red eagle with an arrow in its breast.

Upon hearing these words, the men of the village, both young and old, both heroes and cowards, trimmed new arrows for the contest. At gray dawn there stood indistinct under the shadow of the bluff many human figures; silent as ghosts and wrapped in robes girdled tight about their waists, they waited with chosen bow and arrow.

Some cunning old warriors stayed not with the group. They crouched low upon the open ground. But all eyes alike were fixed upon the top of the high bluff. Breathless they watched for the soaring of the red eagle.

From within the dwellings many eyes peeped through the small holes in the front lapels of the teepee. With shaking knees and hard-set teeth, the women peered out upon the Dakota men prowling about with bows and arrows.

At length when the morning sun also peeped over the eastern horizon at the armed Dakotas, the red eagle walked out upon the edge of the cliff. Pluming his gorgeous feathers, he ruffled his neck and flapped his strong wings together. Then he dived into the air. Slowly he winged his way over the round camp ground; over the men with their strong bows and arrows! In an instant the long bows were bent. Strong straight arrows with red feathered tips sped upward to the blue sky. Ah! slowly moved those indifferent wings, untouched by the poison-beaked arrows. Off to the west beyond the reach of arrow, beyond the reach of eye, the red eagle flew away.

A sudden clamor of high-pitched voices broke the deadly stillness of the dawn. The women talked excitedly about the invulnerable red of the eagle's feathers, while the would-be heroes sulked within their wigwams. "Hĕ-hĕ-hĕ!" groaned the chieftain.

The Tree-Bound

On the evening of the same day sat a group of hunters around a bright burning fire. They were talking of a strange young man whom they spied while out upon a hunt for deer beyond the bluffs. They saw the stranger taking aim. Following the point of his arrow with their eyes, they beheld a herd of buffalo. The arrow sprang from the bow! It darted into the skull of the foremost buffalo. But unlike other arrows it pierced through the head of the creature and spinning in the air lit into the next buffalo head. One by one the buffalo fell upon the sweet grass they were grazing. With straight quivering limbs they lay on their sides. The young man stood calmly by, counting on his fingers the buffalo as they dropped dead to the ground. When the last one fell, he ran thither and picking up his magic arrow wiped it carefully on the soft grass. He slipped it into his long fringed quiver.

"He is going to make a feast for some hungry tribe of men or beasts!" cried the hunters among themselves as they hastened away.

They were afraid of the stranger with the sacred arrow. When the hunter's tale of the stranger's arrow reached the ears of the chieftain, his face brightened with a smile. He sent forth fleet horsemen, to learn of him his birth, his name, and his deeds.

"If he is the avenger with the magic arrow, sprung up from the earth out of a clot of buffalo blood, bid him come hither. Let him kill the red eagle with his magic arrow. Let him win for himself one of my beautiful daughters," he had said to his messengers, for the old story of the badger's man-son was known all over the level lands.

After four days and nights the braves returned. "He is coming," they said. "We

have seen him. He is straight and tall;
handsome in face, with large black eyes.
He paints his round cheeks with bright red,
and wears the penciled lines of red over
his temples like our men of honored rank.
He carries on his back a long fringed
quiver in which he keeps his magic arrow.
His bow is long and strong. He is coming
now to kill the big red eagle." All around
the camp ground from mouth to ear passed
those words of the returned messengers.

Now it chanced that immortal Iktomi,
fully recovered from the brown burnt spots,
overheard the people talking. At once he
was filled with a new desire. "If only
I had the magic arrow, I would kill the
red eagle and win the chieftain's daughter
for a wife," said he in his heart.

Back to his lonely wigwam he hastened.
Beneath the tree in front of his teepee he
sat upon the ground with chin between his
drawn-up knees. His keen eyes scanned

the wide plain. He was watching for the avenger.

"'He is coming!' said the people," muttered old Iktomi. All of a sudden he raised an open palm to his brow and peered afar into the west. The summer sun hung bright in the middle of a cloudless sky. There across the green prairie was a man walking bareheaded toward the east.

"Ha! ha! 't is he! the man with the magic arrow!" laughed Iktomi. And when the bird with the yellow breast sang loud again — "Koda Ni Dakota! Friend, you're a Dakota!" Iktomi put his hand over his mouth as he threw his head far backward, laughing at both the bird and man.

"He is your friend, but his arrow will kill one of your kind! He is a Dakota, but soon he'll grow into the bark on this tree! Ha! ha! ha!" he laughed again.

The Tree-Bound

The young avenger walked with swaying
strides nearer and nearer toward the lonely
wigwam and tree. Iktomi heard the swish!
swish! of the stranger's feet through the
tall grass. He was passing now beyond the
tree, when Iktomi, springing to his feet,
called out: "How, how, my friend! I see
you are dressed in handsome deerskins and
have red paint on your cheeks. You are
going to some feast or dance, may I ask?"
Seeing the young man only smiled Iktomi
went on: "I have not had a mouthful of
food this day. Have pity on me, young
brave, and shoot yonder bird for me!"
With these words Iktomi pointed toward the
tree-top, where sat a bird on the highest
branch. The young avenger, always ready
to help those in distress, sent an arrow
upward and the bird fell. In the next branch
it was caught between the forked prongs.

"My friend, climb the tree and get the
bird. I cannot climb so high. I would

get dizzy and fall," pleaded Iktomi. The avenger began to scale the tree, when Iktomi cried to him : "My friend, your beaded buckskins may be torn by the branches. Leave them safe upon the grass till you are down again."

"You are right," replied the young man, quickly slipping off his long fringed quiver. Together with his dangling pouches and tinkling ornaments, he placed it on the ground. Now he climbed the tree unhindered. Soon from the top he took the bird. "My friend, toss to me your arrow that I may have the honor of wiping it clean on soft deerskin!" exclaimed Iktomi.

"How!" said the brave, and threw the bird and arrow to the ground.

At once Iktomi seized the arrow. Rubbing it first on the grass and then on a piece of deerskin, he muttered indistinct words all the while. The young man, stepping downward from limb to limb, hearing the low muttering, said : " Iktomi, I cannot hear what you say ! "

"Oh, my friend, I was only talking of your big heart."

Again stooping over the arrow Iktomi continued his repetition of charm words. " Grow fast, grow fast to the bark ,of the tree," he whispered. Still the young man moved slowly downward. Suddenly dropping the arrow and standing erect, Iktomi said aloud : " Grow fast to the bark of the tree ! " Before the brave could leap from the tree he became tight-grown to the bark.

" Ah ! ha ! " laughed the bad Iktomi. " I have the magic arrow ! I have the beaded buckskins of the great avenger ! " Hooting and dancing beneath the tree, he said : " I shall kill the red eagle ; I shall wed the chieftain's beautiful daughter ! "

" Oh, Iktomi, set me free ! " begged the tree-bound Dakota brave. But Iktomi's ears were like the fungus on a tree. He did not hear with them.

Wearing the handsome buckskins and carrying proudly the magic arrow in his right hand, he started off eastward. Imitating the swaying strides of the avenger, he walked away with a face turned slightly skyward.

"Oh, set me free! I am glued to the tree like its own bark! Cut me loose!" moaned the prisoner.

A young woman, carrying on her strong back a bundle of tightly bound willow sticks, passed near by the lonely teepee. She heard the wailing man's voice. She paused to listen to the sad words. Looking around she saw nowhere a human creature. "It may be a spirit," thought she.

"Oh! cut me loose! set me free! Iktomi has played me false! He has made me bark of his tree!" cried the voice again.

The Tree-Bound

The young woman dropped her pack of firewood to the ground. With her stone axe she hurried to the tree. There before her astonished eyes clung a young brave close to the tree.

Too shy for words, yet too kind-hearted to leave the stranger tree-bound, she cut loose the whole bark. Like an open jacket she drew it to the ground. With it came the young man also. Free once more, he started away. Looking backward, a few paces from the young woman, he waved his hand, upward and downward, before her face. This was a sign of gratitude used when words failed to interpret strong emotion.

When the bewildered woman reached her dwelling, she mounted a pony and rode swiftly across the rolling land. To the camp ground in the east, to the chieftain troubled by the red eagle, she carried her story.

SHOOTING OF THE RED EAGLE

SHOOTING OF THE RED EAGLE

A MAN in buckskins sat upon the top of
a little hillock. The setting sun shone
bright upon a strong bow in his hand.
His face was turned toward the round
camp ground at the foot of the hill. He
had walked a long journey hither. He
was waiting for the chieftain's men to
spy him.

Soon four strong men ran forth from the
center wigwam toward the hillock, where
sat the man with the long bow.

"He is the avenger come to shoot the
red eagle," cried the runners to each
other as they bent forward swinging their
elbows together.

They reached the side of the stranger,
but he did not heed them. Proud and

silent he gazed upon the cone-shaped wigwams beneath him. Spreading a hand-
somely decorated buffalo robe before the
man, two of the warriors lifted him by
each shoulder and placed him gently on it.
Then the four men took, each, a corner
of the blanket and carried the stranger,
with long proud steps, toward the chieftain's
teepee.

Ready to greet the stranger, the tall chieftain stood at the entrance way. "How, you
are the avenger with the magic arrow!"
said he, extending to him a smooth soft
hand.

"How, great chieftain!" replied the man,
holding long the chieftain's hand. Enter-
ing the teepee, the chieftain motioned the
young man to the right side of the doorway, while he sat down opposite him with
a center fire burning between them. Word-
less, like a bashful Indian maid, the avenger
ate in silence the food set before him on

the ground in front of his crossed shins. When he had finished his meal he handed the empty bowl to the chieftain's wife, saying, " Mother-in-law, here is your dish!"

"Han, my son!" answered the woman, taking the bowl.

With the magic arrow in his quiver the stranger felt not in the least too presuming in addressing the woman as his mother-in-law.

Complaining of fatigue, he covered his face with his blanket and soon within the chieftain's teepee he lay fast asleep.

" The young man is not handsome after all!" whispered the woman in her husband's ear.

" Ah, but after he has killed the red eagle he will seem handsome enough!" answered the chieftain.

That night the star men in their burial procession in the sky reached the low northern horizon, before the center fires

within the teepees had flickered out. The
ringing laughter which had floated up
through the smoke lapels was now hushed,
and only the distant howling of wolves
broke the quiet of the village. But the
lull between midnight and dawn was short
indeed. Very early the oval-shaped door-
flaps were thrust aside and many brown
faces peered out of the wigwams toward
the top of the highest bluff.

Now the sun rose up out of the east.
The red painted avenger stood ready within
the camp ground for the flying of the red
eagle. He appeared, that terrible bird!
He hovered over the round village as if
he could pounce down upon it and devour
the whole tribe.

When the first arrow shot up into the
sky the anxious watchers thrust a hand
quickly over their half-uttered "hinnu!"
The second and the third arrows flew
upward but missed by a wide space the

red eagle soaring with lazy indifference over the little man with the long bow. All his arrows he spent in vain. "Ah! my blanket brushed my elbow and shifted the course of my arrow!" said the stranger as the people gathered around him.

During this happening, a woman on horseback halted her pony at the chieftain's teepee. It was no other than the young woman who cut loose the tree-bound captive!

While she told the story the chieftain listened with downcast face. "I passed him on my way. He is near!" she ended.

Indignant at the bold impostor, the wrathful eyes of the chieftain snapped fire like red cinders in the night time. His lips were closed. At length to the woman he said: "How, you have done me a good deed." Then with quick decision he gave command to a fleet horseman to meet the avenger. "Clothe him in these my best buckskins," said he, pointing to a bundle within the wigwam.

In the meanwhile strong men seized Iktomi and dragged him by his long hair to the hilltop. There upon a mock-pillared grave they bound him hand and feet. Grown-ups and children sneered and hooted at Iktomi's disgrace. For a half-day he lay there, the laughing-stock of the people. Upon the arrival of the real avenger, Iktomi was released and chased away beyond the outer limits of the camp ground.

On the following morning at daybreak, peeped the people out of half-open door-flaps.

There again in the midst of the large camp ground was a man in beaded buck-skins. In his hand was a strong bow and red-tipped arrow. Again the big red eagle appeared on the edge of the bluff. He plumed his feathers and flapped his huge wings.

Shooting of the Red Eagle

The young man crouched low to the ground. He placed the arrow on the bow, drawing a poisoned flint for the eagle.

The bird rose into the air. He moved his outspread wings one, two, three times and lo! the eagle tumbled from the great height and fell heavily to the earth. An arrow stuck in his breast! He was dead!

So quick was the hand of the avenger, so sure his sight, that no one had seen the arrow fly from his long bent bow.

In awe and amazement the village was dumb. And when the avenger, plucking a red eagle feather, placed it in his black hair, a loud shout of 'the people went up to the sky. Then hither and thither ran singing men and women making a great feast for the avenger.

Thus he won the beautiful Indian princess who never tired of telling to her children the story of the big red eagle.

IKTOMI AND THE TURTLE

IKTOMI AND THE TURTLE

The huntsman Patkaša (turtle) stood bent over a newly slain deer.

The red-tipped arrow he drew from the wounded deer was unlike the arrows in his own quiver. Another's stray shot had killed the deer. Patkaša had hunted all the morning without so much as spying an ordinary blackbird.

At last returning homeward, tired and heavy-hearted that he had no meat for the hungry mouths in his wigwam, he walked slowly with downcast eyes. Kind ghosts pitied the unhappy hunter and led him to the newly slain deer, that his children should not cry for food.

When Patkaša stumbled upon the deer in his path, he exclaimed: "Good spirits have pushed me hither!"

Thus he leaned long over the gift of the friendly ghosts.

"How, my friend!" said a voice behind his ear, and a hand fell on his shoulder. It was not a spirit this time. It was old Iktomi.

"How, Iktomi!" answered Patkaša, still stooping over the deer.

"My friend, you are a skilled hunter," began Iktomi, smiling a thin smile which spread from one ear to the other.

Suddenly raising up his head Patkaša's black eyes twinkled as he asked: "Oh, you really say so?"

"Yes, my friend, you are a skillful fellow. Now let us have a little contest. Let us see who can jump over the deer without touching a hair on his hide," suggested Iktomi.

"Oh, I fear I cannot do it!" cried Patkaša, rubbing his funny, thick palms together.

" Have no coward's doubt, Patkaša. I say you are a skillful fellow who finds nothing hard to do." With these words Iktomi led Patkaša a short distance away. In little puffs Patkaša laughed uneasily.

" Now, you may jump first," said Iktomi.

Patkaša, with doubled fists, swung his fat arms to and fro, all the while biting hard his under lip.

Just before the run and leap Iktomi put in : " Let the winner have the deer to eat ! "

It was too late now to say no. Patkaša was more afraid of being called a coward than of losing the deer. " Ho-wo," he replied, still working his short arms. At length he started off on the run. So quick and small were his steps that he seemed to be kicking the ground only. Then the leap ! But Patkaša tripped upon a stick and fell hard against the side of the deer.

"Hĕ-hĕ-hĕ!" exclaimed Iktomi, pretending disappointment that his friend had fallen.

Lifting him to his feet, he said : " Now it is my turn to try the high jump!" Hardly was the last word spoken than Iktomi gave a leap high above the deer.

" The game is mine!" laughed he, patting the sullen Patkaša on the back. " My friend, watch the deer while I go to bring my children," said Iktomi, darting lightly through the tall grass.

Patkaša was always ready to believe the words of scheming people and to do the little favors any one asked of him. However, on this occasion, he did not answer "Yes, my friend." He realized that Iktomi's flattering tongue had made him foolish.

He turned up his nose at Iktomi, now almost out of sight, as much as to say : " Oh, no, Ikto ; I do not hear your words!"

Soon there came a murmur of voices. The sound of laughter grew louder and louder. All of a sudden it became hushed. Old Iktomi led his young Iktomi brood to the place where he had left the turtle, but it was vacant. Nowhere was there any sign of Patkaša or the deer. Then the babes did howl!

"Be still!" said father Iktomi to his children. "I know where Patkaša lives. Follow me. I shall take you to the turtle's dwelling." He ran along a narrow footpath toward the creek near by. Close upon his heels came his children with tear-streaked faces.

"There!" said Iktomi in a loud whisper as he gathered his little ones on the bank. "There is Patkaša broiling venison! There is his teepee, and the savory fire is in his front yard!"

The young Iktomis stretched their necks and rolled their round black eyes like newly hatched birds. They peered into the water.

"Now, I will cool Patkaša's fire. I shall bring you the broïled venison. Watch closely. When you see the black coals rise to the surface of the water, clap your hands and shout aloud, for soon after that sign I shall return to you with some tender meat."

Thus saying Iktomi plunged into the creek. Splash! splash! the water leaped upward into spray. Scarcely had it become leveled and smooth than there bubbled up many black spots. The creek was seething with the dancing of round black things.

"The cooled fire! The coals!" laughed the brood of Iktomis. Clapping together their little hands, they chased one another along the edge of the creek. They shouted and hooted with great glee.

"Āhäš!" said a gruff voice across the water. It was Patkaša. In a large willow tree leaning far over the water he sat upon a large limb. On the very same branch was a bright burning fire over which Patkaša broiled the venison. By this time the water was calm again. No more danced those black spots on its surface, for they were the toes of old Iktomi. He was drowned.

The Iktomi children hurried away from the creek, crying and calling for their water-dead father.

DANCE IN A BUFFALO SKULL

DANCE IN A BUFFALO SKULL

IT was night upon the prairie. Overhead the stars were twinkling bright their red and yellow lights. The moon was young. A silvery thread among the stars, it soon drifted low beneath the horizon.

Upon the ground the land was pitchy black. There are night people on the plain who love the dark. Amid the black level land they meet to frolic under the stars. Then when their sharp ears hear any strange footfalls nigh they scamper away into the deep shadows of night. There they are safely hid from all dangers, they think.

Thus it was that one very black night, afar off from the edge of the level land, out of the wooded river bottom glided forth two

balls of fire. They came farther and farther into the level land. They grew larger
and brighter. The dark hid the body of
the creature with those fiery eyes. They
came on and on, just over the tops of the
prairie grass. It might have been a wildcat prowling low on soft, stealthy feet.
Slowly but surely the terrible eyes drew
nearer and nearer to the heart of the level
land.

There in a huge old buffalo skull was a
gay feast and dance! Tiny little field mice
were singing and dancing in a circle to the
boom-boom of a wee, wee drum. They
were laughing and talking among themselves while their chosen singers sang loud
a merry tune.

They built a small open fire within
the center of their queer dance house.
The light streamed out of the buffalo
skull through all the curious sockets and
holes.

A light on the plain in the middle of the night was an unusual thing. But so merry were the mice they did not hear the "kinš, kinš" of sleepy birds, disturbed by the unaccustomed fire.

A pack of wolves, fearing to come nigh this night fire, stood together a little distance away, and, turning their pointed noses to the stars, howled and yelped most dismally. Even the cry of the wolves was unheeded by the mice within the lighted buffalo skull.

They were feasting and dancing; they were singing and laughing — those funny little furry fellows.

All the while across the dark from out the low river bottom came that pair of fiery eyes.

Now closer and more swift, now fiercer and glaring, the eyes moved toward the buffalo skull. All unconscious of those fearful eyes, the happy mice nibbled at dried roots and venison. The singers had started another song. The drummers beat the time, turning their heads from side to side in rhythm. In a ring around the fire hopped the mice, each bouncing hard on his two hind feet. Some carried their tails over their arms, while others trailed them proudly along.

Ah, very near are those round yellow eyes! Very low to the ground they seem to creep — creep toward the buffalo skull. All of a sudden they slide into the eye-sockets of the old skull.

"Spirit of the buffalo!" squeaked a frightened mouse as he jumped out from a hole in the back part of the skull.

"A cat! a cat!" cried other mice as they scrambled out of holes both large and snug. Noiseless they ran away into the dark.

THE TOAD AND THE BOY

THE TOAD AND THE BOY

THE water-fowls were flying over the marshy lakes. It was now the hunting season. Indian men, with bows and arrows, were wading waist deep amid the wild rice. Near by, within their wigwams, the wives were roasting wild duck and making down pillows.

In the largest teepee sat a young mother wrapping red porcupine quills about the long fringes of a buckskin cushion. Beside her lay a black-eyed baby boy cooing and laughing. Reaching and kicking upward with his tiny hands and feet, he played with the dangling strings of his heavy-beaded bonnet hanging empty on a tent pole above him.

119

At length the mother laid aside her red quills and white sinew-threads. The babe fell fast asleep. Leaning on one hand and softly whispering a little lullaby, she threw a light cover over her baby. It was almost time for the return of her husband.

Remembering there were no willow sticks for the fire, she quickly girdled her blanket tight about her waist, and with a short-handled ax slipped through her belt, she hurried away toward the wooded ravine. She was strong and swung an ax as skillfully as any man. Her loose buckskin dress was made for such freedom. Soon carrying easily a bundle of long willows on her back, with a loop of rope over both her shoulders, she came striding homeward.

Near the entrance way she stooped low, at once shifting the bundle to the right and with both hands lifting the noose from over her head. Having thus dropped the

wood to the ground, she disappeared into
her teepee. In a moment she came running out again, crying, "My son! My little son is gone!" Her keen eyes swept
east and west and all around her. There
was nowhere any sign of the child.

Running with clinched fists to the near-
est teepees, she called: "Has any one seen
my baby? He is gone! My little son is
gone!"

"Hinnú! Hinnú!" exclaimed the women,
rising to their feet and rushing out of their
wigwams.

"We have not seen your child! What
has happened?" queried the women.

With great tears in her eyes the mother
told her story.

"We will search with you," they said
to her as she started off.

They met the returning husbands, who
turned about and joined in the hunt for
the missing child. Along the shore of the

121

lakes, among the high-grown reeds, they looked in vain. He was nowhere to be found. After many days and nights the search was given up. It was sad, indeed, to hear the mother wailing aloud for her little son.

It was growing late in the autumn. The birds were flying high toward the south. The teepees around the lakes were gone, save one lonely dwelling.

Till the winter snow covered the ground and ice covered the lakes, the wailing woman's voice was heard from that solitary wigwam. From some far distance was also the sound of the father's voice singing a sad song.

Thus ten summers and as many winters have come and gone since the strange disappearance of the little child. Every autumn with the hunters came the unhappy parents of the lost baby to search again for him.

The Toad and the Boy

Toward the latter part of the tenth season when, one by one, the teepees were folded and the families went away from the lake region, the mother walked again along the lake shore weeping. One evening, across the lake from where the crying woman stood, a pair of bright black eyes peered at her through the tall reeds and wild rice. A little wild boy stopped his play among the tall grasses. His long, loose hair hanging down his brown back and shoulders was carelessly tossed from his round face. He wore a loin cloth of woven sweet grass. Crouching low to the marshy ground, he listened to the wailing voice. As the voice grew hoarse and only sobs shook the slender figure of the woman, the eyes of the wild boy grew dim and wet.

At length, when the moaning ceased, he sprang to his feet and ran like a nymph with swift outstretched toes. He rushed into a small hut of reeds and grasses.

"Mother! Mother! Tell me what voice it was I heard which pleased my ears, but made my eyes grow wet!" said he, breathless.

"Han, my son," grunted a big, ugly toad. "It was the voice of a weeping woman you heard. My son, do not say you like it. Do not tell me it brought tears to your eyes. You have never heard me weep. I can please your ear and break your heart. Listen!" replied the great old toad.

Stepping outside, she stood by the entrance way. She was old and badly puffed out. She had reared a large family of little toads, but none of them had aroused her love, nor ever grieved her. She had heard the wailing human voice and marveled at the throat which produced the strange sound. Now, in her great desire to keep the stolen boy awhile longer, she ventured to cry as the Dakota woman does. In a gruff, coarse voice she broke forth:

"Hin-hin, doe-skin! Hin-hin, Ermine, Ermine! Hin-hin, red blanket, with white border!"

Not knowing that the syllables of a Dakota's cry are the names of loved ones gone, the ugly toad mother sought to please the boy's ear with the names of valuable articles. Having shrieked in a torturing voice and mouthed extravagant names, the old toad rolled her tearless eyes with great satisfaction. Hopping back into her dwelling, she asked:

"My son, did my voice bring tears to your eyes? Did my words bring gladness to your ears? Do you not like my wailing better?"

"No, no!" pouted the boy with some impatience. "I want to hear the woman's voice! Tell me, mother, why the human voice stirs all my feelings!"

The toad mother said within her breast, "The human child has heard and seen his real mother. I cannot keep him longer, I fear. Oh, no, I cannot give away the pretty creature I have taught to call me 'mother' all these many winters."

"Mother," went on the child voice, "tell me one thing. Tell me why my little brothers and sisters are all unlike me."

The big, ugly toad, looking at her pudgy children, said: "The eldest is always best."

This reply quieted the boy for a while. Very closely watched the old toad mother her stolen human son. When by chance he started off alone, she shoved out one of her own children after him, saying: "Do not come back without your big brother."

Thus the wild boy with the long, loose hair sits every day on a marshy island hid among the tall reeds. But he is not alone. Always at his feet hops a little toad brother. One day an Indian hunter, wading in the deep waters, spied the boy. He had heard of the baby stolen long ago.

The Toad and the Boy

"This is he!" murmured the hunter to himself as he ran to his wigwam. "I saw among the tall reeds a black-haired boy at play!" shouted he to the people.

At once the unhappy father and mother cried out, "'T is he, our boy!" Quickly he led them to the lake. Peeping through the wild rice, he pointed with unsteady finger toward the boy playing all unawares.

"'T is he! 't is he!" cried the mother, for she knew him.

In silence the hunter stood aside, while the happy father and mother caressed their baby boy grown tall.

IYA, THE CAMP–EATER

IYA, THE CAMP-EATER

FROM the tall grass came the voice of a crying babe. The huntsmen who were passing nigh heard and halted.

The tallest one among them hastened toward the high grass with long, cautious strides. He waded through the growth of green with just a head above it all. Suddenly exclaiming "Hunhe!" he dropped out of sight. In another instant he held up in both his hands a tiny little baby, wrapped in soft brown buckskins.

"Oh ho, a wood-child!" cried the men, for they were hunting along the wooded river bottom where this babe was found.

While the hunters were questioning whether or no they should carry it home, the wee Indian baby kept up his little howl.

"His voice is strong!" said one.

"At times it sounds like an old man's voice!" whispered a superstitious fellow, who feared some bad spirit hid in the small child to cheat them by and by.

"Let us take it to our wise chieftain," at length they said; and the moment they started toward the camp ground the strange wood-child ceased to cry.

Beside the chieftain's teepee waited the hunters while the tall man entered with the child.

"How! how!" nodded the kind-faced chieftain, listening to the queer story. Then rising, he took the infant in his strong arms; gently he laid the black-eyed babe in his daughter's lap. "This is to be your little son!" said he, smiling.

"Yes, father," she replied. Pleased with the child, she smoothed the long black hair fringing his round brown face.

"Tell the people that I give a feast and dance this day for the naming of

132

my daughter's little son," bade the chieftain.

In the meanwhile among the men waiting by the entrance way, one said in a low voice: "I have heard that bad spirits come as little children into a camp which they mean to destroy."

"No! no! Let us not be overcautious. It would be cowardly to leave a baby in the wild wood where prowl the hungry wolves!" answered an elderly man.

The tall man now came out of the chieftain's teepee. With a word he sent them to their dwellings half running with joy.

"A feast! a dance for the naming of the chieftain's grandchild!" cried he in a loud voice to the village people.

"What? what?" asked they in great surprise, — holding a hand to the ear to catch the words of the crier.

There was a momentary silence among the people while they listened to the ringing voice of the man walking in the center ground. Then broke forth a rippling, laughing babble among the cone-shaped teepees. All were glad to hear of the chieftain's grandson. They were happy to attend the feast and dance for its naming. With excited fingers they twisted their hair into glossy braids and painted their cheeks with bright red paint. To and fro hurried the women, handsome in their gala-day dress. Men in loose deerskins, with long tinkling metal fringes, strode in small numbers toward the center of the round camp ground.

Here underneath a temporary shade-house of green leaves they were to dance and feast. The children in deerskins and paints, just like their elders, were jolly little men and women. Beside their eager parents they skipped along toward the green dance house.

Here seated in a large circle, the people were assembled, the proud chieftain rose with the little baby in his arms. The noisy hum of voices was hushed. Not a tinkling of a metal fringe broke the silence. The crier came forward to greet the chieftain, then bent attentively over the small babe, listening to the words of the chieftain. When he paused the crier spoke aloud to the people:

"This woodland child is adopted by the chieftain's eldest daughter. His name is Chaske. He wears the title of the eldest son. In honor of Chaske the chieftain gives this feast and dance! These are the words of him you see holding a baby in his arms."

"Yes! Yes! Hinnu! How!" came from the circle. At once the drummers beat softly and slowly their drum while the chosen singers hummed together to find the common pitch. The beat of the drum grew louder and faster. The singers burst forth in a lively tune. Then the drumbeats subsided and faintly marked the rhythm of the singing. Here and there bounced up men and women, both young and old. They danced and sang with merry light hearts. Then came the hour of feasting.

Late into the night the air of the camp ground was alive with the laughing voices of women and the singing in unison of young men. Within her father's teepee sat the chieftain's daughter. Proud of her little one, she watched over him asleep in her lap.

Gradually a deep quiet stole over the camp ground, as one by one the people fell into pleasant dreams. Now all the village was still. Alone sat the beautiful young mother watching the babe in her lap, asleep with a gaping little mouth. Amid the quiet of the night, her ear heard the far-off hum of many voices. The faint sound of murmuring people was in the air. Upward she glanced at the smoke hole of the wigwam and saw a bright star peeping down upon her. "Spirits in the air above?" she wondered. Yet there was no sign to tell her of their nearness. The fine small sound of voices grew larger and nearer.

"Father! rise! I hear the coming of some tribe. Hostile or friendly — I cannot tell. Rise and see!" whispered the young woman.

"Yes, my daughter!" answered the chieftain, springing to his feet.

Though asleep, his ear was ever alert. Thus rushing out into the open, he listened for strange sounds. With an eagle eye he scanned the camp ground for some sign.

Returning he said: "My daughter, I hear nothing and see no sign of evil nigh."

"Oh! the sound of many voices comes up from the earth about me!" exclaimed the young mother.

137

Bending low over her babe she gave ear to the ground. Horrified was she to find the mysterious sound came out of the open mouth of her sleeping child!

"Why so unlike other babes!" she cried within her heart as she slipped him gently from her lap to the ground. "Mother, listen and tell me if this child is an evil spirit come to destroy our camp!" she whispered loud.

Placing an ear close to the open baby mouth, the chieftain and his wife, each in turn heard the voices of a great camp. The singing of men and women, the beating of the drum, the rattling of deer-hoofs strung like bells on a string, these were the sounds they heard.

"We must go away," said the chieftain, leading them into the night. Out in the open he whispered to the frightened young woman: "Iya, the camp-eater, has come in the guise of a babe. Had you gone to

138

sleep, he would have jumped out into his own shape and would have devoured our camp. He is a giant with spindling legs. He cannot fight, for he cannot run. He is powerful only in the night with his tricks. We are safe as soon as day breaks." Then moving closer to the woman, he whispered: "If he wakes now, he will swallow the whole tribe with one hideous gulp! Come, we must flee with our people."

Thus creeping from teepee to teepee a secret alarm signal was given. At midnight the teepees were gone and there was left no sign of the village save heaps of dead ashes. So quietly had the people folded their wigwams and bundled their tent poles that they slipped away unheard by the sleeping Iya babe.

When the morning sun arose, the babe awoke. Seeing himself deserted, he threw off his baby form in a hot rage.

Wearing his own ugly shape, his huge body toppled to and fro, from side to side, on a pair of thin legs far too small for their burden. Though with every move he came dangerously nigh to falling, he followed in the trail of the fleeing people.

"I shall eat you in the sight of a noon-day sun!" cried Iya in his vain rage, when he spied them encamped beyond a river.

By some unknown cunning he swam the river and sought his way toward the teepees.

"Hin! hin!" he grunted and growled. With perspiration beading his brow he strove to wiggle his slender legs beneath his giant form.

"Ha! ha!" laughed all the village people to see Iya made foolish with anger. "Such spindle legs cannot stand to fight by day-light!" shouted the brave ones who were terror-struck the night before by the name "Iya."

140

Warriors with long knives rushed forth and slew the camp-eater.

Lo! there rose out of the giant a whole Indian tribe: their camp ground, their tee-pees in a large circle, and the people laughing and dancing.

" We are glad to be free! " said these strange people.

Thus Iya was killed ; and no more are the camp grounds in danger of being swallowed up in a single night time.

MANŠTIN, THE RABBIT

MANŠTIN, THE RABBIT

MANŠTIN was an adventurous brave, but very kind-hearted. Stamping a moccasined foot as he drew on his buckskin leggins, he said: "Grandmother, beware of Iktomi! Do not let him lure you into some cunning trap. I am going to the North country on a long hunt."

With these words of caution to the bent old rabbit grandmother with whom he had lived since he was a tiny babe, Manštin started off toward the north. He was scarce over the great high hills when he heard the shrieking of a human child.

"Wän!" he ejaculated, pointing his long ears toward the direction of the sound; "Wän! that is the work of cruel Double-

Face. Shameless coward! he delights in torturing helpless creatures!"

Muttering indistinct words, Manštin ran up the last hill and lo! in the ravine beyond stood the terrible monster with a face in front and one in the back of his head!

This brown giant was without clothes save for a wild-cat-skin about his loins. With a wicked gleaming eye, he watched the little black-haired baby he held in his strong arm. In a laughing voice he hummed an Indian mother's lullaby, "Ä-bōō! Äbōō!" and at the same time he switched the naked baby with a thorny wild-rose bush.

Quickly Manštin jumped behind a large sage bush on the brow of the hill. He bent his bow and the sinewy string twanged. Now an arrow stuck above the ear of Double-Face. It was a poisoned arrow, and the giant fell dead. Then Manštin took the little brown baby and hurried away from the ravine. Soon he came to a teepee from whence loud wailing voices broke. It was the teepee of the stolen baby and the mourners were its heart-broken parents.

When gallant Manstin returned the child to the eager arms of the mother there came a sudden terror into the eyes of both the Dakotas. They feared lest it was Double-Face come in a new guise to torture them. The rabbit understood their fear and said: "I am Manstin, the kind-hearted,— Manstin, the noted huntsman. I am your friend. Do not fear."

That night a strange thing happened. While the father and mother slept, Manstin took the wee baby. With his feet placed gently yet firmly upon the tiny toes of the little child, he drew upward by each small hand the sleeping child till he was a full-grown man. With a forefinger he traced a slit in the upper lip; and when on the

147

morrow the man and woman awoke they could not distinguish their own son from Manŝtin, so much alike were the braves.

"Henceforth we are friends, to help each other," said Manŝtin, shaking a right hand in farewell. "The earth is our common ear, to carry from its uttermost extremes one's slightest wish for the other!"

"Ho! Be it so!" answered the newly made man.

Upon leaving his friend, Manŝtin hurried away toward the North country whither he was bound for a long hunt. Suddenly he came upon the edge of a wide brook. His alert eye caught sight of a rawhide rope staked to the water's brink, which led away toward a small round hut in the distance. The ground was trodden into a deep groove beneath the loosely drawn rawhide rope.

"Hun-hĕ!" exclaimed Manŝtin, bending over the freshly made footprints in the

moist bank of the brook. "A man's footprints!" he said to himself. "A blind man
lives in yonder hut! This rope is his guide
by which he comes for his daily water!"
surmised Manstin, who knew all the peculiar contrivances of the people. At once
his eyes became fixed upon the solitary
dwelling and hither he followed his curi-
osity, — a real blind man's rope.

Quietly he lifted the door-flap and entered
in. An old toothless grandfather, blind and
shaky with age, sat upon the ground. He
was not deaf however. He heard the
entrance and felt the presence of some
stranger.

"How, grandchild," he mumbled, for he
was old enough to be grandparent to every
living thing, "how! I cannot see you.
Pray, speak your name!"

"Grandfather, I am Manstin," answered
the rabbit, all the while looking with
curious eyes about the wigwam.

"Grandfather, what is it so tightly packed in all these buckskin bags placed against the tent poles?" he asked.

"My grandchild, those are dried buffalo meat and venison. These are magic bags which never grow empty. I am blind and cannot go on a hunt. Hence a kind Maker has given me these magic bags of choicest foods."

Then the old, bent man pulled at a rope which lay by his right hand. "This leads me to the brook where I drink! and this," said he, turning to the one on his left, "and this takes me into the forest, where I feel about for dry sticks for my fire."

"Grandfather, I wish I lived in such sure luxury! I would lean back against a tent pole, and with crossed feet I would smoke sweet willow bark the rest of my days," sighed Manstin.

"My grandchild, your eyes are your luxury! you would be unhappy without them!" the old man replied.

"Grandfather, I would give you my two eyes for your place!" cried Manstin.

"How! you have said it. Arise. Take out your eyes and give them to me. Henceforth you are at home here in my stead."

At once Manstin took out both his eyes and the old man put them on! Rejoicing, the old grandfather started away with his young eyes while the blind rabbit filled his dream pipe, leaning lazily against the tent pole. For a short time it was a most pleasant pastime to smoke willow bark and to eat from the magic bags.

Manstin grew thirsty, but there was no water in the small dwelling. Taking one of the rawhide ropes he started toward the brook to quench his thirst. He was young and unwilling to trudge slowly in the old man's footpath. He was full of glee, for it had been many long moons since he had tasted such good food. Thus he skipped confidently along jerking the old weather-eaten rawhide spasmodically till all of a sudden it gave way and Manŝtin fell head-long into the water.

"Ĕn! Ĕn!" he grunted kicking frantic-ally amid stream. All along the slippery bank he vainly tried to climb, till at last he chanced upon the old stake and the deeply worn footpath. Exhausted and inwardly disgusted with his mishaps, he crawled more cautiously on all fours to his wig-wam door. Dripping with his recent plunge he sat with chattering teeth within his unfired wigwam.

The sun had set and the night air was chilly, but there was no fire-wood in the dwelling. "Hin!" murmured Manŝtin and bravely tried the other rope. "I go for some fire-wood!" he said, following the rawhide rope which led into the forest. Soon he stumbled upon thickly strewn dry willow sticks. Eagerly with both hands he gathered the wood into his outspread blanket. Manstin was naturally an energetic fellow.

When he had a large heap, he tied two opposite ends of blanket together and lifted the bundle of wood upon his back, but alas! he had unconsciously dropped the end of the rope and now he was lost in the wood!

"Hin! hin!" he groaned. Then pausing a moment, he set his fan-like ears to catch any sound of approaching footsteps. There was none. Not even a night bird twittered to help him out of his predicament.

With a bold face, he made a start at random.

He fell into some tangled wood where he was held fast. Manstin let go his bundle and began to lament having given away his two eyes.

"Friend, my friend, I have need of you! The old oak tree grandfather has gone off with my eyes and I am lost in the woods!" he cried with his lips close to the earth.

Scarcely had he spoken when the sound of voices was audible on the outer edge of the forest. Nearer and louder grew the voices — one was the clear flute tones of a young brave and the other the tremulous squeaks of an old grandfather.

It was Manstin's friend with the Earth Ear and the old grandfather. "Here Manstin, take back your eyes," said the old man, "I knew you would not be content in my stead, but I wanted you to learn your lesson. I have had pleasure seeing with your eyes and trying your bow and arrows, but since I am old and feeble I much prefer my own teepee and my magic bags!"

Thus talking the three returned to the hut. The old grandfather crept into his wigwam, which is often mistaken for a mere oak tree by little Indian girls and boys.

Manstin, with his own bright eyes fitted into his head again, went on happily to hunt in the North country.

THE WARLIKE SEVEN

THE WARLIKE SEVEN

ONCE seven people went out to make war,— the Ashes, the Fire, the Bladder, the Grasshopper, the Dragon Fly, the Fish, and the Turtle. As they were talking excitedly, waving their fists in violent gestures, a wind came and blew the Ashes away. "Ho!" cried the others, "he could not fight, this one!"

The six went on running to make war more quickly. They descended a deep valley, the Fire going foremost until they came to a river. The Fire said "Hsss— tchu!" and was gone. "Ho!" hooted the others, "he could not fight, this one!"

Therefore the five went on the more quickly to make war. They came to a great wood. While they were going through it, the Bladder was heard to sneer and to say, "Hĕ! you should rise above these, brothers." With these words he went upward among the tree-tops; and the thorn apple pricked him. He fell through the branches and was nothing! "You see this!" said the four, "this one could not fight."

Still the remaining warriors would not turn back. The four went boldly on to make war. The Grasshopper with his cousin, the Dragon Fly, went foremost. They reached a marshy place, and the mire was very deep. As they waded through the mud, the Grasshopper's legs stuck, and he pulled them off! He crawled upon a log and wept, "You see me, brothers, I cannot go!"

The Dragon Fly went on, weeping for his cousin. He would not be comforted, for he loved his cousin dearly. The more he grieved, the louder he cried, till his body shook with great violence. He blew his red swollen nose with a loud noise so that his head came off his slender neck, and he was fallen upon the grass.

"You see how it is," said the Fish, lashing his tail impatiently, "these people were not warriors!" "Come!" he said, "let us go on to make war."

Thus the Fish and the Turtle came to a large camp ground.

"Ho!" exclaimed the people of this round village of teepees, "Who are these little ones? What do they seek?"

Neither of the warriors carried weapons with them, and their unimposing stature misled the curious people.

The Fish was spokesman. With a peculiar omission of syllables, he said: "Shu . . . hi pi!"

"Wän! what? what?" clamored eager voices of men and women.

Again the Fish said: "Shu . . . hi pi!" Everywhere stood young and old with a palm to an ear. Still no one guessed what the Fish had mumbled!

From the bewildered crowd witty old Iktomi came forward. "Hĕ, listen!" he shouted, rubbing his mischievous palms together, for where there was any trouble brewing, he was always in the midst of it.

"This little strange man says, 'Zuya unhipi! We come to make war!'"

"Ūun!" resented the people, suddenly stricken glum. "Let us kill the silly pair! They can do nothing! They do not know the meaning of the phrase. Let us build a fire and boil them both!"

"If you put us on to boil," said the Fish, "there will be trouble."

"Ho ho!" laughed the village folk. "We shall see."

And so they made a fire.

"I have never been so angered!" said the Fish. The Turtle in a whispered reply said: "We shall die!"

When a pair of strong hands lifted the Fish over the sputtering water, he put his mouth downward. "Whssh!" he said. He blew the water all over the people, so that many were burned and could not see. Screaming with pain, they ran away.

"Oh, what shall we do with these dreadful ones?" they said.

Others exclaimed: "Let us carry them to the lake of muddy water and drown them!"

Instantly they ran with them. They threw the Fish and the Turtle into the lake. Toward the center of the large lake the Turtle dived. There he peeped up out of the water and, waving a hand at the crowd, sang out, "This is where I live!"

The Fish swam hither and thither with such frolicsome darts that his back fin made the water fly. "Ĕ han!" whooped the Fish, "this is where I live!"

"Oh, what have we done!" said the frightened people, "this will be our undoing."

Then a wise chief said: "Iya, the Eater, shall come and swallow the lake!"

So one went running. He brought Iya, the Eater; and Iya drank all day at the lake till his belly was like the earth. Then the Fish and the Turtle dived into the mud; and Iya said: "They are not in me." Hearing this the people cried greatly.

Iktomi wading in the lake had been swallowed like a gnat in the water. Within the great Iya he was looking skyward. So deep was the water in the Eater's stomach that the surface of the swallowed lake almost touched the sky.

"I will go that way," said Iktomi, looking at the concave within arm's reach.

He struck his knife upward in the Eater's stomach, and the water falling out drowned those people of the village.

Now when the great water fell into its own bed, the Fish and the Turtle came to the shore. They went home painted victors and loud-voiced singers.